Innovative language teaching and learning at university: a look at new trends

Edited by Nelson Becerra, Rosalba Biasini,
Hanna Magedera-Hofhansl, and Ana Reimão

research-publishing.net

Published by Research-publishing.net, a not-for-profit association
Voillans, France, info@research-publishing.net

© 2019 by Editors (collective work)
© 2019 by Authors (individual work)

Innovative language teaching and learning at university: a look at new trends
Edited by Nelson Becerra, Rosalba Biasini, Hanna Magedera-Hofhansl, and Ana Reimão

Publication date: 2019/05/06

Rights: the whole volume is published under the Attribution-NonCommercial-NoDerivatives International (CC BY-NC-ND) licence; **individual articles may have a different licence**. Under the CC BY-NC-ND licence, the volume is freely available online (https://doi.org/10.14705/rpnet.2019.32.9782490057368) for anybody to read, download, copy, and redistribute provided that the author(s), editorial team, and publisher are properly cited. Commercial use and derivative works are, however, not permitted.

Disclaimer: Research-publishing.net does not take any responsibility for the content of the pages written by the authors of this book. The authors have recognised that the work described was not published before, or that it was not under consideration for publication elsewhere. While the information in this book is believed to be true and accurate on the date of its going to press, neither the editorial team nor the publisher can accept any legal responsibility for any errors or omissions. The publisher makes no warranty, expressed or implied, with respect to the material contained herein. While Research-publishing.net is committed to publishing works of integrity, the words are the authors' alone.

Trademark notice: product or corporate names may be trademarks or registered trademarks, and are used only for identification and explanation without intent to infringe.

Copyrighted material: every effort has been made by the editorial team to trace copyright holders and to obtain their permission for the use of copyrighted material in this book. In the event of errors or omissions, please notify the publisher of any corrections that will need to be incorporated in future editions of this book.

Typeset by Research-publishing.net
Cover design by © Raphaël Savina (raphael@savina.net)

ISBN13: 978-2-490057-36-8 (Ebook, PDF, colour)
ISBN13: 978-2-490057-37-5 (Ebook, EPUB, colour)
ISBN13: 978-2-490057-35-1 (Paperback - Print on demand, black and white)
Print on demand technology is a high-quality, innovative and ecological printing method; with which the book is never 'out of stock' or 'out of print'.

British Library Cataloguing-in-Publication Data.
A cataloguing record for this book is available from the British Library.

Legal deposit, UK: British Library.
Legal deposit, France: Bibliothèque Nationale de France - Dépôt légal: mai 2019.

Table of contents

v   Notes on contributors

xvi   Acknowledgements

1   New trends in language teaching and learning at university: an introduction
Nelson Becerra, Rosalba Biasini, Hanna Magedera-Hofhansl, and Ana Reimão

Section 1. Keynote speakers

9   Paradox 2018: diversification of learners, contexts, and modes of delivery necessitates application of universal learning principles
Hitomi Masuhara

19   From new literacies to transmedia literacies: the New Approaches to Transmedia and Languages Pedagogy project
Carmen Herrero

Section 2. Active learning and student empowerment

29   Supporting and empowering language teachers through action research communities
Angela Gallagher-Brett

37   Independent reading together – combining self-directed and collaborative learning
Theresa Federici

45   Process drama and theatre in the learning of Italian. The case of 'I Promessi sposi di Birmingham, un "romanzo criminale"'
Fabrizio Di Maio

53   The European University Tandem project – an integrated online platform to foster intercultural language exchanges across Europe (and beyond)
Anke Bohm, Veronika Koeper-Saul, and Christian Mossmann

Table of contents

63 Becoming a more active and creative language learner with digital tools
Mikiko Kurose

73 Incorporating D2L and Google Docs in language teaching and learning
Miao Li

83 Challenging, supporting, and empowering students in IWLP beginners'classes: a teaching and learning response to internationalisation
Alison Nader

95 Improving feedback through computer-based language proficiency assessment
Tania Horák and Elena Gandini

105 Student-led grammar revision: empowering first year Spanish beginner students to facilitate their own learning
Nadezhda Bonelli and Anna Nibbs

115 Awareness poster campaign for the development of presentation skills in Spanish
Elia Lorena López

123 Author index

Notes on contributors

1. Editors

Nelson Becerra is Lecturer in Latin American Spanish Language and Culture at the University of Liverpool. He studied at the UPTC Colombia before moving to England where he studied an MA in Economics and Social Studies and an MPhil in Latin American Studies, both at the University of Manchester. His research interests include technology enhanced learning, translation in the undergraduate curriculum and Latin American Spanish and culture. He has recently developed the LACSE project, a student exchange using technology between universities in the UK, Latin America, and Spain, to prepare students for the year abroad, enhance cultural awareness, and improve linguistic skills.

Rosalba Biasini is Lecturer in Italian at the University of Liverpool where she has been teaching Italian language and culture at all levels since 2013. She graduated in Lettere Classiche/Classics (L'Aquila, Italy, 2004). She holds an MA in Translation Studies (Manchester 2005), a PhD/D.Phil. in Italian (Oxford, 2010), and a Master ITALS – Didactics of Italian as a Foreign Language (Ca' Foscari, Venice, 2013). Her research interests and publications span from literature of the Italian Resistance to didactics of Italian as a foreign language, with a focus on the use of translation and of digital tools.

Hanna Magedera-Hofhansl, born in France, and raised in Austria, did a degree in French, Portuguese, and Lutheran Theology at the universities of Vienna and Strasbourg. After working at the French Cultural Institute in Vienna, she came to the University of Liverpool in 2001 and is now a lecturer in German language. Her special focus in teaching is intercultural communication translation, employability, and transferable skills.

Ana Reimão is Lecturer in Portuguese Studies at the University of Liverpool, where since 2005 she has taught Portuguese from absolute beginners to advanced levels as well thematic units on Lusophone literature. She is a founding member of TROPO UK – the Association of Teachers and Researchers of Portuguese which encourages scholarly research and promotes good practice on aspects of learning and teaching Portuguese in order to support the professional

Notes on contributors

development of teachers. She is also an enthusiastic organiser of events such as concerts, film screenings, and translation slams, in order to enable learning beyond the walls of the classroom.

2. Reviewers

Ana Bela Almeida is Lecturer in Portuguese language and culture in the Modern Languages and Cultures Department at the University of Liverpool. Ana Bela is one of the co-founders of the Litinclass – "Literature in the Foreign Language Class" international research network, which was created to explore and share ideas on the ways literature can enhance language learning. Ana Bela was awarded a University of Liverpool Learning and Teaching Award in 2016 and co-authored a publication in Research-publishing.net. Currently, Ana Bela is co-organising the Literature in Language Learning Conference 2019, which will take place at the University of Liverpool in June 2019.

Carmen Álvarez-Mayo, BA, PGCE, MA, CMALT, is Philologist and works at the University of York where she is Lecturer in the Department of Language and Linguistic Science and a member of the University Learning and Teaching Forum Committee. Carmen is a Certified Member of the Association for Learning Technology (CMALT) and in terms of teaching is particularly interested in the promotion of student-centred active learning fostering discussion and reflection through innovative, varied, and inclusive work and assessment that will allow students to develop creativity, intercultural competency, interdisciplinarity, and employability skills. Carmen sometimes works as a translator, interpreter, editor, and voice over actor, and has worked at Instituto Cervantes and Leeds Beckett University.

Lida Amiri, with her comparative study of contemporary translingual authors of Afghanistani background titled 'Rethinking World Literature and Diasporic Writing: the Case of Afghanistani Translingual Authors Khaled Hosseini and Atiq Rahimi', researches alternative diaspora narratives published in English, French, and Persian. Lida Amiri obtained her Master's degree in literary and linguistic studies at the University of Wuppertal and was awarded various scholarships ranging from Fulbright to Friedrich-Ebert-Stiftung to Deutscher Akademischer Austauschdienst to study at Université de la Sorbonne Nouvelle (Paris III) and also gain teaching experiences as Foreign Language Teaching Assistant at Webster University and the University of Melbourne.

Dorit Fellner, after acquiring a Master's degree in German, English, and Scandinavian philology at The University of Vienna and specialising in German as a foreign language, moved to the UK in February 2001. After some years of teaching at high schools, and then also at an infant and junior school, she began to teach at the Language Centre as a part-time tutor. In September 2012, she became the Senior Language Tutor for German and Dutch and the Exam Officer for the Goethe Examination Centre. Since then she has also been an external examiner at two other universities and UniLang assessor since October 2016.

Teresa Franco studied Italian Literature at the University of Rome, La Sapienza, and completed a D.Phil. in Medieval and Modern Languages at the University of Oxford in 2013. She is currently Language Lector in Italian at the University of Oxford and Fellow of the Higher Education Academy. Her research interests span from literary translation, to the reception of foreign texts, and women's authorship in 20th century Italy. She also writes for the cultural supplement of the Italian newspaper Il Sole 24 Ore.

Blanca González-Valencia, from Pamplona (Spain), has a BA in Humanities (University of Navarra), a PGCE (University of Navarra), a BA in English Studies (University of Zaragoza), and an MA in Translation Studies (University of Salford) and several courses focussed on the teaching of Spanish as a Foreign Language. She has previous experience teaching Spanish as a Foreign Language at Salford University and Aston University. Her research interests are Audiovisual Translation, Translation, and contextualisation in the FL classroom and the adaptation of audiovisual products. She is currently working and doing a PhD at the University of Manchester entitled 'Dubbing Ken Loach's Anti-austerity Narratives in Spanish: I, Daniel Blake as a Case Study'.

Notes on contributors

Dr Caterina Guardamagna is Lecturer in English Language/Linguistics at the University of Liverpool. Her background is in cognitive-functional historical linguistics. Her PhD research dealt with the development of secundum NP ("according to NP") in Latin. More recently, Dr Guardamagna has developed an interest in historical pragmatics, especially (im)politeness in Latin, multilingual practices in Early Modern English, with particular attention to Shakespeare versus his contemporaries, and corpus assisted discourse analysis of citizenship in Early Modern Britain.

Sofia Martinho is Associate Professor of Portuguese at the University of Leeds where she is the Director of the Camões Centre for Portuguese Language and teaches Portuguese and Lusophone Literatures and Cultures. Before joining the University of Leeds in 2008, she was the Director of the Camões Centre in Goa (India) and at the University of Newcastle (UK). Her scholarship focusses in the areas of Digital Literacies for Language Learning, Uses, and Effectiveness of Technologies in Language Learning and Teaching and Online Autonomous Language Learning. Her most recent project explores effective ways to develop MFL Speaking Skills at UG level. Since 2017, Sofia is the President of TROPO-UK the Association of Researchers and Teachers of Portuguese Language in the UK.

Isabel Molina-Vidal has a degree in Translation and Interpretation at the University of Alicante (Spain) and MA in Technology, Education, and Learning at the University of Leeds. She has been teaching Spanish as a foreign language since 2003. From 2004 to 2012 she was Head of studies and teacher of Spanish as a foreign language at the Language School Estudio Sampere in Alicante (Spain). Since 2013 she is working at Instituto Cervantes Mánchester-Leeds as teacher of Spanish as a foreign language and teacher trainer. She is also teaching courses of Spanish language and culture at the University of Leeds and the University of Huddersfield from 2014 to 2018. She has published the paper "Thinking the Grammar: Teaching a cognitive grammar in a blended-learning context" in the Language Scholar at the University of Leeds. She is currently working as a Spanish Lecturer at the University of Leeds.

Notes on contributors

Dr Marina Mozzon-McPherson is Professor of Innovation in Language Learning and Teaching in the Faculty of Arts and Social Sciences at the University of Hull. Her research broadly embraces three specific areas of applied linguistics and language education: language as a pedagogic and cultural mediation tool; creative learning spaces (multicultural, multilingual environments; virtual worlds etc.); and construction of learning communities and communities of practice (face-to-face, online in informal settings). She leads a new interdisciplinary research cluster, Chinese Whispers, which examines the transformative synergies between language learning and intercultural understanding through music.

Helga Müllneritsch is a PhD student at the University of Liverpool. Her thesis focusses on the manuscript cookery book in the long eighteenth century: its materiality, its function, and female authorship, and ownership. Her publications in the history of food and cookery include 'The Chameleon in the Kitchen: The Plural Identities of the Manuscript "Cookery Book"', in Annie Linnéa Mattsson, Helga Müllneritsch, and Eve Rosenhaft (eds.), The Materiality of Writing: Manuscript Practices in the Age of Print (Uppsala 2019), and 'The 'Who' of Manuscript Recipe Books: Tracing Professional Scribes', in Sjuttonhundratal: Nordic Yearbook for Eighteenth-Century Studies (2017).

Dr José Peixoto Coelho de Souza teaches Portuguese at the University of Manchester, in England. He has a PhD in Applied Linguistics and a BA in English and English language literature from the Federal University of Rio Grande do Sul, in Brazil. His research interests include language teaching materials development, the use of songs in language teaching, Portuguese as an Additional Language teaching, and literomusical literacy. He has presented papers and taught workshops and short courses on those subjects to pre-service and in-service teachers in Brazil, Colombia, Portugal, Spain, and in the United Kingdom.

Dr Lei Peng joined the University of Liverpool in 2016 and has been working as Lecturer in Chinese Studies at Modern Languages and Cultures department since then. She has successfully completed a PhD in Transcultural Studies in

Notes on contributors

2014 and has been teaching Chinese Mandarin as a foreign language for over ten years in the higher education both in France and UK. Sharing her knowledge and understanding while learning new things with and from others has always been a source of satisfaction for her. Her research interests are broadly focussed on modern Chinese social transformation and cultural history, especially concerning the alternative music culture in contemporary China.

Anna Proudfoot is Head of Italian in the School of Languages and Applied Linguistics at the Open University. She developed print and online materials for the Beginners' Italian and Intermediate Italian modules and also contributes to the MA in Translation. She is currently Lead Educator on the OU-Future Learn Italian for Beginners' MOOCs, and in 2018 collaborated with the BBC on the programme Rome Unpacked. Anna has published several Italian grammar and language learning texts. Her research focusses on student engagement in online language learning.

Marina Rabadán-Gómez graduated in English Studies (Universidad de Huelva, Spain, 2002), has an MA in education (Universidad de Huelva, Spain, 2004), an MA in Applied Linguistics (Universitat de Barcelona Spain, 2012), and is currently working on her PhD thesis on the development of the pragmatic competence in students of Spanish as a Foreign Language (ELE). She is Lecturer in Spanish at the University of Liverpool since 2014 and her research interests span from teaching materials development and teacher training, with a focus on L2 pragmatics, to Public Service Interpreting training.

Jordi Sánchez is Lecturer of Spanish at the University of Liverpool since 2014, teaching undergraduate students to advanced students in their first year. He has an extensive experience teaching Spanish and Catalan as a foreign language at the Instituto Cervantes in Manchester and at the Manchester Metropolitan University. He also has taught proficiency courses on different topics related to Spain and Latin America in the aforementioned institutions. At the present he is researching on the use of the technology for learning and teaching purposes as well as the use of flipped classroom in higher education. He is a member of ALT, Chartered Institute of Linguists (CIOL), UK ELE, and accredited examiner for UNILANG.

Notes on contributors

Federica Sturani moved to the UK soon after graduating in Modern Languages at the University of Macerata, Italy, to teach Italian at the University of Manchester, UK, where she obtained an MPhil on Italian television adaptation of classic novels. During her career she also worked at Liverpool John Moores University and the University of Central Lancashire in Preston. Her long standing interest in Italian language teaching lead to several publications for the Teach Yourself series, including "Italian Tutor. Grammar and Vocabulary workbook". She is currently University Teacher at Liverpool University and Associate Lecturer at Edge Hill University, Ormskirk.

3. Authors

Anke Bohm is the current DAAD Lecturer in German in the Department of Modern Languages and Cultures at the University of Liverpool, employability lead, and student engagement officer for the department. She has taught German in Spain, Switzerland, and the UK in different institutional contexts. Her interests include flipped classroom approaches to teaching grammar and second language acquisition.

Nadezhda Bonelli is a specialist in teaching Spanish as a foreign language to undergraduates and adults. She has worked for various UK Higher Education institutions, delivering face-to-face and online courses. She has also worked on early childhood bilingual education, the subject of her M.Ed dissertation. Nadezhda combines the findings of her studies and various teaching methods to create innovative language teaching projects with the local community. She currently coordinates the Spanish beginners' language course at the University of Sheffield.

Dr Fabrizio Di Maio has studied in Rome, BA in Humanities, and Paris Sorbonne, MA in Comparative Literature. In 2010 he completed a PhD in Italian Studies (University of Rome 2) and he is completing a PhD in Modern Languages at the University of Birmingham (2019). He has worked at the University of Gabès, Grenoble 1, Grenoble 3, and Birmingham. He publishes on 20th and 21st

Notes on contributors

Century Italian literature, with a particular focus on the relations between history and literature.

Theresa Federici is Lecturer in the School of Modern Languages at Cardiff University. Her research interests are enquiry-based learning and process-driven approaches to materials design. She is interested in learner identity in foreign language acquisition and the impact of teaching materials on students' sense of integration into the L2 community.

Angela Gallagher-Brett is Head of Learning and Teaching Development at SOAS, University of London, where she leads a team of staff working in academic development, technology-enhanced learning, and student retention and success. She is Senior Fellow of the Higher Education Academy and has a PhD in Applied Linguistics. Her research interests focus on language learning and teaching motivation, action research, and employability in the curriculum. She has worked on UK-wide and international education development projects.

Elena Gandini is an EFL/ESOL lecturer at the UCLan, teaching on EFL and EAP courses, contributing to test development as a member of the language testing team, and working on pre-service teacher training intensive courses. She has previously worked as a teacher, examiner, and teacher trainer in Italy, Austria, and Germany. Her research interests are in the area of language testing and assessment, multilingualism, and material development.

Carmen Herrero is Principal Lecturer in the Department of Languages, Information, and Communications at Manchester Metropolitan University, UK. She co-founded the Film in Language Teaching Association (www.filta.org.uk) and is the director of the research group Film, Languages and Media in Education (www2.mmu.ac.uk/languages/flame/). Carmen has published widely on Spanish film and language teaching, including the co-edited volume Using Film and Media in the Language Classroom: Reflections on Research-led Teaching (Multilingual Matters 2019). ORCID: https://orcid.org/0000-0002-1392-4224

Notes on contributors

Dr Tania Horák is Senior Lecturer at UCLan (UK) teaching on EFL teacher training programmes. She is currently course leader of MA in TESOL and applied linguistics. She has previously worked in the field of English language teaching in the Czech Republic, Bangladesh, Lithuania, Hong Kong, and Germany. Her research interests lie in foreign language testing and assessment, above all washback, impact, and social consequences of assessment.

Veronika Koeper-Saul is Lecturer in German in the Department of Modern Languages and Cultures at the University of Liverpool, Erasmus Coordinator for German, and Modern Languages Resources Manager in the University's Language Lounge. Her interests include approaches to independent learning, intercultural exchange, and teaching culture in the foreign language classroom.

Mikiko Kurose is Teaching Associate at the University of Nottingham, where she teaches Japanese from beginners to intermediate level. She previously taught Japanese in a state secondary school for 13 years where she taught up to A-level before moving into higher education. Her research interests are technology integration and enhancement in language teaching and learning, and the benefits of CEFR in teaching and assessment.

Miao Li is French Instructor at the School of Languages, Linguistics, Literatures and Cultures, University of Calgary, Canada. She holds a PhD in French literature from Queen's University in Kingston, Canada. Her research interests include China and Chinese in the 18th century French literature, women's writing in the 18th century French literature, and the use of technology in foreign language teaching and learning. Previously, Miao worked as French and Chinese Instructor in Mount Royal University, Canada.

Dr Elia Lorena López is Associate Lecturer in the Department of Language and Linguistic Science at the University of York since 2012. She is the Coordinator of the Spanish Degree Programme and previous roles have included the Coordination of the Languages for All (LFA) Spanish provision as part of the University's Institute-Wide Language Programme (IWLP). Her pedagogy is based on the concept of "authentic assessment" and on the

Notes on contributors

integration of Academic and Professional Skills (APS) for language learning. Fellow of the Higher Education Academy (HEA) since 2015. Co-organiser of INNOCONF16.

Dr Hitomi Masuhara is Secretary of Materials Development Association (www.matsda.org), HEA Fellow, and an ex-Director of the MAs Applied Linguistics and TESOL in the Department of English in the University of Liverpool. She was Project Leader of the HEFCE Minority Subject funding, co-ordinating 20 Lesser Taught Languages. She won Innovation and Leadership Chancellor's Award and the LTSN grant for her work 'The Cultural Twist', teacher, and materials development project on incorporating cultural awareness in language teaching. For other information see http://www.liv.ac.uk/english/staff/hitomi-masuhara/.

Christian Mossmann is Lecturer in German in the Department of Modern Languages at the University of Exeter and Language Coordinator for German in the university's Foreign Language Centre. His research interests include medium of instruction policies in higher education, intercultural learning, and innovative approaches to language teaching. From 2015 to 2017 he was the Exeter Project Lead for the EU-funded European University Tandem (EUniTa) project.

Alison Nader is IWLP Lecturer at The University of Reading's International Study and Language Institute. She developed an interest in communicative language teaching working with adult learners and has also coordinated the IWLP French team before becoming the School Director of Teaching and Learning. Working with adult learners and non-specialist home and international university students, Alison developed an interest and expertise in teaching students from diverse backgrounds; meeting their needs both in class and through differentiated materials development. Recent projects include work on assessment and feedback and developing speaking and listening materials.

Anna Nibbs is an academic developer, enterprise and entrepreneurship education specialist, and Senior Fellow of the Higher Education Academy. She has held roles supporting learning and teaching since 2002, and her experiences of higher education teaching and curriculum development span eight and ten years respectively. Anna is Learning and Teaching Enhancement Adviser at The University of Sheffield, and was a founding member of the National Enterprise Educator Award-winning University of Sheffield Enterprise Academy.

Acknowledgements

We would like to thank the University of Liverpool's School of Histories, Languages, and Cultures (HLC) and the Centre for Teaching Excellence in Language Learning (CTELL) for their generous financial contribution towards the organisation of the conference and the publication of this volume, as well as our sponsors Sanako, Hueber, European Schoolbooks, and Research-publishing.net.

We would also like to thank the speakers and delegates for making InnoConf 2018 a very enriching and fulfilling day, the organisers of previous conferences for their on-going advice, and all the reviewers who contributed with their time and knowledge to this publication.

We would like to further extend our gratitude to Emma Hoey, in the HLC Marketing, Recruitment, and Events team for her dedication and endless support; Karine Fenix from Research-publishing.net for her help and infinite patience; Ulrike Bavendiek, director of CTELL, for her continued support; Kristyan Spelman-Miller, Dean of Education at the Faculty of Humanities and Social Sciences of the University of Liverpool, for her time and words of encouragement; and finally to all colleagues in MLC for their advice and help on the day of the conference. A further special mention goes to Jordi Sánchez-Carrión for his multi-media coverage of the event.

Nelson Becerra, Rosalba Biasini, Hanna Magedera-Hofhansl, and Ana Reimão

1 New trends in language teaching and learning at university: an introduction

Nelson Becerra[1], Rosalba Biasini[2], Hanna Magedera-Hofhansl[3], and Ana Reimão[4]

1. Background

InnoConf 2018 – the Innovative Language Teaching and Learning at University Conference – took place at the University of Liverpool in June 2018 and focussed on the theme of 'New Trends in Language Teaching and Learning at University'. Since 2010, InnoConfs have been successfully organised across the UK and most have had a focus on specific themes such as enhancing employability, integrating informal learning into formal language education, and enhancing participation and collaboration. Rather than focussing on a set area, the InnoConf 2018 committee chose a broad theme in order to continue to give delegates the opportunity to reflect on best practice in the sector while at the same time capturing the state of the art of language teaching and learning.

InnoConf 2018 welcomed over 90 delegates from different countries, including the speakers who delivered four workshops, 24 papers, and four posters on teaching modern foreign languages as well as English as a foreign language.

---

1. University of Liverpool, Liverpool, England; nelson.becerra@liverpool.ac.uk

2. University of Liverpool, Liverpool, England; rosalba.biasini@liverpool.ac.uk

3. University of Liverpool, Liverpool, England; hofhansl@liverpool.ac.uk

4. University of Liverpool, Liverpool, England; a.reimao@liverpool.ac.uk

How to cite this chapter: Becerra, N., Biasini, R., Magedera-Hofhansl, H., & Reimão, A. (2019). New trends in language teaching and learning at university: an introduction. In N. Becerra, R. Biasini, H. Magedera-Hofhansl & A. Reimão (Eds), *Innovative language teaching and learning at university: a look at new trends* (pp. 1-5). Research-publishing.net. https://doi.org/10.14705/rpnet.2019.32.396

Chapter 1

2. Keynote speakers

Carmen Herrero (Manchester Metropolitan University) opened the day with a keynote titled *From new literacies to transmedia literacies: fostering participatory cultures in language learning and teaching in higher education*. Hitomi Masuhara (University of Liverpool) ended the day with a keynote titled *Paradox 2018: diversification points to universal learning principles*. Both keynote speakers reflected on the challenges presented by teaching foreign languages in the context of higher education. Herrero described her research project on enhancing language skills through the development of transmedia literacy, and Masuhara focussed on the importance of adopting universal learning principles when designing teaching and learning activities and materials.

In her paper, included in this volume, **Masuhara** identifies four challenges in teaching and learning foreign languages and recognises that these could trigger new teaching trends. She recommends that to ensure the quality and effectiveness of provision as well as to satisfy the needs of a diverse body of learners, teachers abide to the suggested principles.

We can read **Herrero**'s paper, also included in this volume, as a response to some of these challenges. Herrero recognises the nature of current ways of engaging with information, especially for the under 30's, highlighting the importance of incorporating these practices into language teaching and learning in order to foster meaningful participation in a multi-modal digital world.

There were many engaging communications throughout the day on topics such as employability and outreach, student support and inclusion, scaffolded learning, inclusion of international students and global connectivity, assessment and feedback, technology-enhanced learning, and digital skills. The Innoconf 2018 committee are pleased to include a selection of these communications below in the form of short papers and case studies. The overarching trait that emerged from these was 'active learning and student empowerment'.

3. Active learning and student empowerment

In line with this idea, we open with **Gallagher-Brett**'s paper on empowering teachers in the belief that teachers serve as role models for students in their journey towards active learning. This paper is slightly anomalous within this volume because it does not describe classroom practices. Instead, Gallagher-Brett reports on a project that promotes action research in order to establish participatory clusters and communities of teachers who use this methodology to survey and review their practice.

Following from this, **Federici**'s paper on independent and collaborative reading details the experience of giving students of Italian autonomy in choosing reading materials. Among the benefits of this approach are increased learner confidence and motivation alongside improved language skills and cultural awareness. The paper sets a clear rationale for the methodology used as well as clear guidance for anyone wishing to adopt a similar approach.

Di Maio's paper is another example of enhancing students' engagement and motivation. He analyses the use of process drama and theatre in the Italian class. In their diversity, process drama and theatre promote different learning experiences. After briefly describing these methods, Di Maio explores his teaching practice, reflecting on how both process drama and theatre can enrich the student experience and foster a creative and imaginative use of the foreign language.

We them move into examples of using technology-enhanced learning. **Bohm**, **Koeper-Saul**, and **Mossmann**, who were involved in building the EU-funded platform EUniTa, discuss language learning via this online tandem exchange. Their paper explores how this platform offers students learning opportunities that enhance reciprocal and autonomous learning in German, English, Spanish, French, and Italian. Through authentic communication enhanced by the use of specifically designed learning materials, the platform aims to foster students' *basic interpersonal communication skills* and *cognitive academic language proficiency*. **Kurose** provides a further insight on how to incorporate digital tools into teaching in order to tackle the issue of low participation and interaction. This paper describes the benefits of learning language through tasks, thus enabling students to overcome ingrained passive-learner behaviour. The author argues that students became more motivated while working collaboratively and took ownership of their learning. Similarly, **Li** explores the effectiveness of the use of the virtual learning environment platform Desire2Learn and of Google Docs in helping learners and teachers in and outside of the classroom. Li maintains that providing an inclusive and interactive learning space creates an active and learner-centred environment.

Dealing with the challenges of internationalisation, **Nader** discusses the experience of learners in institution-wide language programmes. The paper looks at the strategies employed in a Beginners' French module such as adjustments in syllabus, differentiation in assessment, and response to feedback, used to enable the teachers to support learners who might have dropped out or become discouraged. **Horák** and **Gandini** make the case for a better use of feedback in placement tests that would prove equally beneficial to home and international students. The paper discusses findings which emerged when considering moving language level tests to an online platform. The authors suggest an approach that would encourage washback and washforward as the incidental advantages of what was initially a commercially motivated project. At the date of publication, it is still unclear whether this tool will come to fruition. However, Horák and Gandini's account is an insightful reflection on the process and useful to anyone looking into optimising the learning experience through feedback or testing.

To close the volume, we offer two papers on the theme of enhancing employability. **Bonelli** and **Nibbs**'s paper presents a project-based learning activity meant to support beginner language students of Spanish. The activity consists of an optional formative exercise for which students prepare and deliver presentations on key aspects of the Spanish language firstly to their classmates, and subsequently to Year 9 to Year 12 students in local schools, responding to requirements developed collaboratively by school teachers and their language tutor. Also aiming to enhance presentation, teamwork, and time management skills, **López**' paper shows how to embed employability skills in language classes. The author describes a set of activities in which students had to design a poster for a social awareness campaign, including a slogan and hashtag, after which they needed to pitch their product to their peers in a class presentation. Lopez demonstrates how this approach helps develop transferable soft skills as well as enriched language skills.

The present volume is a collection of works that we believe will be of use to language teachers and practitioners in higher education and beyond. InnoConfs have secured a space in the academic calendar of language teachers as an opportunity to exchange ideas and good practice as well as to inspire reflection and create collaborations. This has proven beneficial to bring together early career researchers as well as established scholars, and we hope to have captured this inclusive spirit in this volume.

Section 1.
Keynote speakers

2. Paradox 2018: diversification of learners, contexts, and modes of delivery necessitates application of universal learning principles

Hitomi Masuhara[1]

Abstract

The current challenges for languages in higher education may be summarised as: global and local socio-political changes; diversity of learners with different life-long and life-wide needs and wants; demands for effectiveness, accountability, and employability of our language provision; different modes of delivery at different times and forms; and digital and non-digital delivery and quality assurance. Depending on the individual learners, learning and teaching contexts and modes of delivery, teaching materials and approaches will be different. When we conduct a systematic evaluation of available commercial materials, regardless of their trendy disguises, they tend to be reincarnated clones of popular coursebooks based on traditional syllabuses that assume face-to-face classroom delivery. These materials may come with additional digital materials but they seem to focus on the mechanical aspects of language (e.g. quizzes of discrete item knowledge). How can we ensure the quality and effectiveness of our provision as well as satisfy the diverse learner needs and wants when using different modes of delivery? Whatever approaches we decide to take, the answer paradoxically emerges from our wisdom and efforts in the adaptation and development of materials based on fundamental and universal learning principles that reflect current understanding in second language acquisition.

Keywords: challenges, trends, materials, learning principles.

1. University of Liverpool, Liverpool, England; hitomi@liverpool.ac.uk; https://orcid.org/0000-0001-9625-8206

How to cite this chapter: Masuhara, H. (2019). Paradox 2018: diversification of learners, contexts, and modes of delivery necessitates application of universal learning principles. In N. Becerra, R. Biasini, H. Magedera-Hofhansl & A. Reimão (Eds), *Innovative language teaching and learning at university: a look at new trends* (pp. 9-17). Research-publishing.net. https://doi.org/10.14705/rpnet.2019.32.897

Chapter 2

1. Introduction

In higher education, departments of modern languages as well as of English seem to be facing four main challenges that could trigger new trends in language teaching and learning. The InnoConf 2018 proceedings provide examples of how tutors are trying to ensure quality and innovation in language provision. I believe that the learning principles set out in this paper could work as a compass for navigating forward in a rough higher education language sea.

2. Challenges

2.1. Challenge 1: from 'Inner Circle' English to Global Englishes

Since the 1980's, English has attracted much attention as the most likely lingua franca across the world. 'Inner circle countries' (Kachru, 1985) in which English is used as the native language benefited as places to learn, and where research in English language learning takes place and where materials are produced. Based on thorough analyses of global and local trends in demography, economy, technology, and education, however, Graddol (2006) predicts 'Global Englishes' will take over as the basic medium of international communication. Note here that Global Englishes place priority on intelligible and effective communication among interlocutors with various cultural, religious, and ethnic backgrounds in contrast with the traditional 'inner circle' English. The so called 'native-speaker norm' is merely one of many varieties. The problem is that existing materials and assessment are based on the old paradigm of native-speaker norms and may no longer be meeting the needs/wants of users of Global Englishes.

2.2. Challenge 2: multilingualism

Graddol (2006) also predicted that there would be growing demands for education 'beyond English' in order to maintain the advantage in international, economic, technological, and cultural competition. Studies such as Bel Habib (2011) show how language skills in the workforce could determine gain or loss in business opportunities which are by no means always in English. The dominance of English on the Internet is gradually declining and the cyberspace is shared with lesser-taught languages such as Arabic, Chinese, Portuguese, Russian, and Japanese, as well as less widely taught modern languages such as Spanish (Young, 2015; Zuckerman, 2013). The report *Languages for the Future - Which languages the UK needs most and why* by the British Council (Tinsley & Board, 2013) identifies top ten languages, such as Spanish, Arabic, French, Chinese, and German. EU countries have been making concerted efforts for multilingual education as seen in the works by the European Centre for Modern Languages of the Council of Europe[2].

The UK government's multilingual policy has not been consistent, but recent series of UK government publications and research funding made available (e.g. AHRC Open World Initiative Fund) seem to encourage multilingual education and community language learning. The increasing demand and Brexit may add to the existing challenge of finding teaching staff who have expertise in teaching/learning/assessing as well as language competence in modern languages, including lesser-taught languages.

2.3. Challenge 3: learners

The increasing marketisation of higher education in the UK seems to be fuelling demands for more accountability, employability, and effectiveness in our provision and our delivery modes. Learners from different stages of life-long learning come with their diverse personal, social, and professional needs and/or wants and expect high-quality, relevant, and meaningful content, and highly effective teaching approaches and results (e.g. better career prospects).

The learners also seem to welcome choices of different kinds of learning modes and time requirements, which may sometimes be described as 'life-wide' learning. It may mean synchronous or combined/blended engagement in any kind of learning activities, including formal education in universities or colleges,

---
2. https://www.ecml.at/Home/ProfessionalNetworkForum/tabid/137/Default.aspx

Chapter 2

work-based professional development, community adult education, like-minded communities of people sharing voluntary learning and self-directed learning. The level of access to digital learning adds to the diversification.

2.4. Challenge 4: digital and non-digital materials and quality assurance

With the growth of multilingual Internet communication, digital translation seems to be attracting much attention. We see not only small translator hardware or phone apps for audio/script translation, but also smart multilingual earphones. With the advancement of technology, there may be a day when every day transactions will not require investment of time and effort in learning foreign languages. The necessity, however, would remain for a small number of professionals with high level competence in translation/interpretation/cultural awareness with whatever extra skills required (e.g. diplomacy, business, research).

In the 'Challenge 3: learners' section above, I discussed different delivery methods that may be in demand, such as traditional face-to-face, blended learning, and Massive Open Online Course (MOOC) type autonomous learning with or without certificates. Castaño Muñoz, Redecker, Vuorikari, and Punie (2013)[3], and Redecker (2014)[4] describe how EU countries are preparing for a future open learning environment 2030 that will ensure quality in any possible provisions. The plan involves various service providers including higher education institutions and community-based learning environments. It also envisages purely digital autonomous learning with or without guidance.

3. New trends

The undercurrent of the four challenges I have discussed so far may be summarised as diversification of learners, learning and teaching contexts, and

---

3. See also https://blogs.ec.europa.eu/openeducation2030/ and http://www.lifewideeducation.uk/lifewide-learning.html

4. Also http://www.learninglives.co.uk/uploads/1/0/8/4/10842717/future_of_learning.pdf and http://www.lifewideeducation.uk/

modes of delivery. The crucial question is how we might ensure quality and validity in whatever provisions we offer to specific learners in whatever modes of delivery. Digital materials, for example, are abundant but validity and quality are not guaranteed.

According to various evaluation studies in English language teaching (Masuhara, Mishan, & Tomlinson, 2017; Tomlinson, 2008; Tomlinson & Masuhara, 2013), the most prevalent curricula, materials, and assessments seem to be based on traditional linguistic syllabus, methodology (e.g. Presentation, Practice, and Production, or PPP), and assessment of knowledge and some skills. The materials may claim that they follow the Common European Framework of Reference specifications, but multi-strand course maps reveal that the syllabus is in fact grammar-based with some additional skills and communication related sections.

The answer to the diversification, paradoxically, might emerge from our wisdom and efforts in the adaptation and development of materials based on fundamental and universal learning principles that reflect current understanding in second language acquisition.

Tomlinson (2013a) articulates principles based on his literature survey of Second Language Acquisition (SLA) studies and his own experience (see also Ellis, 2005). Tomlinson (2013) maps out the connections between principles of SLA, teaching, and materials development. Tomlinson (2013a, pp.12-15) lists the following principles:

- a rich and meaningful exposure to language in use;

- an effective and cognitive engagement;

- being allowed to focus on meaning;

- making use of those mental resources typically used in communication in the L1;

- noticing how the L2 is used;

- being given opportunities for contextualised and purposeful communication in the L2; and

- being encouraged to interact.

These principles can be turned into evaluation criteria (e.g. to what extent do the materials provide rich exposure to language in use) and be used to evaluate and adapt existing materials or to develop new materials with approaches such as Task Based (e.g. Masuhara, 2015; Van Den Branden, 2006), Text-Driven (Tomlinson, 2013b), Self-Access (e.g. Cooker, 2008), or Mobile Learning (Reinders & Pegrum, 2016).

SLA researchers seem to agree that language acquisition requires a good amount of implicit learning (i.e. naturalistic, incidental exposure to language in use while focused on meaning), but also some explicit learning (i.e. learners pay motivated attention to linguistic elements in a meaning-focussed context in order to achieve refinement in accurate and appropriate use of language, e.g. Ellis, 2016). Implicit learning may be achieved through, for example, extensive listening (e.g. Renandya & Farrell, 2011), extensive reading (e.g. Maley, 2008), or shared reading (e.g. Ghosn, 2013).

Explicit learning could take place when the learners have focussed on meaningful output (e.g. a draft of a presentation or of communicative writing) and are ready to discover features of language and its use with or without facilitating interventions (e.g. feedback).

Note here that explicit learning is different from explicit teaching that often features in commercially available coursebooks. Coursebooks seem to be mostly concerned with linguistic knowledge and coverage of a syllabus. Their methodology tends to be PPP that provides 'Focus on Forms' (i.e. explicitly teaching linguistic items in an isolated decontextualised manner). SLA researchers differentiate Focus on Form (i.e. learner paying conscious attention to language in use in a meaning focussed context) and Focus on Forms, and recommend the former.

4. Conclusion

I would like to end on a philosophical note. Syllabi, curriculums, materials, and assessments seem to be currently dominated by utilitarian approaches to language teaching in which language is treated as a mere object to be taught, practised, and assessed. In order for language provisions to be relevant and inspiring for the learners, should we not remember why we learn languages in the first place? As the novelist Elena Ferrante (2018) puts it:

> "A language is a compendium of the history, geography, material and spiritual life, the vices and virtues, not only of those who speak it, but also of those who have spoken it through the centuries. The words, the grammar, the syntax are a chisel that shapes our thought" (para. 2).

In this sense, we may like to ensure the quality of input and methodology for the sake of self-actualisation through genuine communication of our thoughts and feelings in language provisions.

References

Bel Habib, I. (2011). Multilingual skills provide export benefits and better access to new emerging markets – multilingual market communication among Swedish, Danish, German and French small and medium sized enterprises. *Sens-Public.* http://www.sens-public.org/spip.php?article869&lang=en#

Castaño Muñoz, J., Redecker, C., Vuorikari, R., & Punie, Y. (2013). Open education 2030: planning the future of adult learning in Europe. *Open Learning, 28*(3), 171-186. https://doi.org/10.1080/02680513.2013.871199

Cooker, L. (2008). Self-access materials. In B. Tomlinson (Ed.), *English learning materials - A critical review* (pp. 110-132). Continuum.

Ellis, R. (2005). Principles of instructed language learning. *System, 33*(2), 209-224. https://doi.org/10.1016/j.system.2004.12.006

Ellis, R. (2016). Focus on form: a critical review. *Language Teaching Research, 20*(3), 405-428. https://doi.org/10.1177/1362168816628627

Ferrante, E. (2018, February 24). Yes, I'm Italian – but I'm not loud, I don't gesticulate and I'm not good with pizza. *The Guardian*. https://www.theguardian.com/lifeandstyle/2018/feb/24/elena-ferrante-on-italian-language-identity

Ghosn, I. (2013). *Storybridge to second language literacy: the theory, research, and practice of teaching English with children's literature*. Information Age Publishing, INC.

Graddol, D. (2006). *English next - why global English may mean the end of 'English as a foreign language'*. The British Council.

Kachru, B. B. (1985). Standards, codification, and sociolinguistic realism: the English language in the outer circle. In R. Quirk & H. Widdowson (Eds), *English in the world: teaching and learning the language and the literature*. Cambridge University Press.

Maley, A. (2008). Extensive reading – maid in waiting. In B. Tomlinson (Ed.), *English language learning materials - a critical view* (pp. 133-156). Continuum International Publishing Group.

Masuhara, H. (2015). 'Anything goes' in task-based language teaching materials? – the need for principled materials evaluation, adaptation and development. *The European Journal of Applied Linguistics and TEFL, 2*, 113-127.

Masuhara, H., Mishan, F., & Tomlinson, B. (Eds). (2017). *Practice and theory for materials development in L2 learning*. Cambridge Scholars Publishing.

Redecker, C. (2014). The future of learning is lifelong, lifewide and open. *Lifewide Magazine, 9*, 12-17.

Reinders, H., & Pegrum, M. (2016). Supporting language learning on the move. In B. Tomlinson (Ed.), *SLA research and materials development for language learning* (pp. 219-231). Routledge.

Renandya, W. A., & Farrell, T. S. (2011). 'Teacher, the tape is too fast!' Extensive listening in ELT. *ELT Journal, 65*(1), 52-59. https://doi.org/10.1093/elt/ccq015

Tinsley, T., & Board, K. (2013). *Languages for the future - which languages the UK needs most and why*. The British Council. https://www.britishcouncil.org/sites/default/files/languages-for-the-future-report.pdf

Tomlinson, B. (Ed.). (2008). *English language learning materials - a critical review*. Continuum.

Tomlinson, B. (2010). Principles of effective materials development. In N. Harwood (Ed.), *English language teaching materials -theory and practice* (pp. 81-108). Cambridge University Press.

Tomlinson, B. (2013a). Second language acquisition and materials development. In B. Tomlinson (Ed.), *Applied linguistics and materials development* (pp. 11-29). Bloomsbury.

Tomlinson, B. (2013b). Developing principled frameworks for materials development. In B. Tomlinson (Ed.), *Developing materials for language teaching* (2nd ed., pp. 95-118). Bloomsbury.

Tomlinson, B., & Masuhara, H. (2013). Adult coursebooks. *ELT Journal, 67*(2), 233-249. https://doi.org/10.1093/elt/cct007

Van den Branden, K. (Ed.). (2006). *Task-based language education*. Cambridge University Press.

Young, H. (2015, May 28). The digital language divide. *The Guardian Supported by the British Academy*. http://labs.theguardian.com/digital-language-divide/

Zuckerman, E. (2013). *English is no longer the language of the web*. https://qz.com/96054/english-is-no-longer-the-language-of-the-web/

3 From new literacies to transmedia literacies: the New Approaches to Transmedia and Languages Pedagogy project

Carmen Herrero[1]

Abstract

As students are becoming avid online media consumers and creators, participatory culture has shifted the focus of literacy from one of individual expression to one of community involvement (Chan & Herrero, 2010, p. 10). Taking into consideration the challenges and opportunities derived from the integration in formal settings (secondary and higher education) of different forms of participatory culture, this article presents the *New Approaches to Transmedia and Languages Pedagogy* project, developed by Manchester Metropolitan University, which has been motivated by the shift towards multimodal forms of communication and representation and the potential of new technologies to engage in more interactive and meaningful forms of learning and teaching. This research project seeks new avenues to supplement L2 teaching using film and video games as well as integrating transmedia and cross-media projects.

Keywords: cross-media, new media, transmedia, participatory culture, L2 learning and teaching.

---

1. Manchester Metropolitan University, Manchester, England; c.herrero@mmu.ac.uk; https://orcid.org/0000-0002-1392-4224

How to cite this chapter: Herrero, C. (2019). From new literacies to transmedia literacies: the New Approaches to Transmedia and Languages Pedagogy project. In N. Becerra, R. Biasini, H. Magedera-Hofhansl & A. Reimão (Eds), *Innovative language teaching and learning at university: a look at new trends* (pp. 19-26). Research-publishing.net. https://doi.org/10.14705/rpnet.2019.32.898

© 2019 Carmen Herrero (CC BY)

Chapter 3

1. Introduction

It is well known that higher education is in the midst of a transformative realignment related to funding and viable business models, developing knowledge, skills, and accreditation. The field of language studies is not immune to the dynamics of the convergent forces driving this metamorphosis. Due to the increasing linguistic, cultural and social diversity, cross-cultural and intercultural approaches permeate language educational policies. Moreover, the employability value of languages has been reiterated by the research findings of the British Academy's study Born Global (British Academy, 2016) and the Future of Work Report (Bakhshi, Downing, Osborne, & Schneider, 2017).

However, despite the evident merit of learning a second language, the diminishing popularity of languages in secondary schools and sixth-form colleges since the late 1990s and early 2000s has accentuated the drop in uptake of language degrees in UK. Yet this trend is not unique to British universities. A recent multi-authored feature in the Times Higher Education, with contributions from modern linguists from/in Australia, Denmark, the UK, and the US, looked at the new shape of the discipline. After weighing the challenges and priorities that can lead to recruiting more students for modern language courses at university level, these scholars offer a wide range of proposals ranging from growing a research-led discipline (Forsdick, 2017) to "communicating to the wider public the value of languages and cultural studies" (Verstraete-Hansen, 2017, n.p.).

Other contributors to the Times Higher Education feature point out the need to revise curricula content. Gramling (2017) proposes offering relevant courses "grounded in the lived complexity of societal multilingualism" (n.p.) and Kelly's (2017) article invites reflection on finding ways for providing an attractive and inspiring curriculum for current and future students who are more familiar with popular forms of culture (cinema, graphic novels, and videogames) than classic literature.

2. The New Approaches to Transmedia and Languages Pedagogy project

In the light of the above recommendations – particularly those calling for language learning tasks and projects that are not detached from real-life needs, interests, and preferences of the students – it is pertinent to note that traditional conventions of literacy have become "anachronistic" in the new communication environment (Kalantzis, Cope, Chan, & Dalley-Trim, 2015, p. 1). This article presents an on-going research project that addresses these issues in L2 teaching and learning. The Manchester Metropolitan University research project *New Approaches to Transmedia and Language Pedagogy* (http://transmediaineducation.com/) is developing a framework for the successful integration of suitable cultural media artefacts and cross-media and transmedia projects in the L2 classroom. This project aims at demonstrating the strategic importance of language-led research, and echoes the importance of multidisciplinary research in a multilingual world.

This project has two research lines. The first one focusses on teacher training and builds on relevant practice and research in the fields of film/visual and multimodal literacies applied to L2 learning and teaching carried out by the researchers through the Film in Language Teaching Association (FILTA[2]) and the research group Film, Languages, And Media in Education (FLAME[3]) at Manchester Metropolitan University in 2013[4]. This sub-project aims to evaluate current practices, curriculum requirements, and teacher training needs regarding the use of visual and media culture in language teaching in secondary schools and higher education in the UK. One of the most relevant conclusions from the literature review is that, moving beyond a monomodal and monolingual understanding of language learning and teaching, a growing body of scholarship is demonstrating the benefits of exploiting the interconnections between different modalities (aural, oral, and visual) in multilingual contexts

---

2. www.filta.org.uk

3. https://www2.mmu.ac.uk/languages/flame/

4. The main characteristic of multimodal texts (e.g. films, video games, or websites) is that they combine written linguistic modes with other patterns of meaning (oral, visual, audio, gestural, tactile, and/or spatial) (Kress & van Leeuwen, 2001).

(Chan & Herrero, 2010; Domínguez Romero, Bobkina, & Stefanova, 2018; Herrero, 2019; Herrero & Vanderschelden, 2019; Kern, 2003; Paesani, Allen, & Dupuy, 2016). As a part of the project, a series of surveys was conducted among secondary and higher education language teachers regarding the views of professional learning in the field of film and moving images applied to language learning and teaching and on the use of short films in L2. Based on the information gathered in the survey, the researchers created open resources centred on the development of intercultural competence, critical thinking/ writing and film analysis, which were piloted in different workshops and IN-SErvice Training days (INSETs). The study guides are available on the Transmedia in Education website.

Henry Jenkins (2006) uses the term *participatory culture* to explain the growth of user-generated content; *distributed cognition* and *collective intelligence*. This new ethos is permeating the development of new literacy strategies in education as demonstrated in Jenkins et al.'s (2009) white paper. Jenkins's (2006) study identifies a series of participatory practices, and new media skills in which youth are engaged nowadays: *play, performance, simulation, appropriation, multitasking, distributed cognition, collective intelligence, judgment, transmedia navigation, networking,* and *negotiation*. In an era of convergence, one of the most relevant skills for the world of education is *transmedia navigation,* defined as "the ability to deal with the flow of stories and information across multiple modalities" (Jenkins et al., 2009, p. 46). The other line of the *New Approaches to Transmedia and Language Pedagogy* project focusses on how transmedia literacy moves forward the concept of new media literacies. An indication of the relevance of this interdisciplinary field is the European funded project *Transmedia Literacy*[5], which has focussed on the media activities that young people (12-18 years old) use in an informal environment and how they can serve to support formal learning in the classroom (Scolari, 2018). However, the review of literature in transmedia literacy in L2 learning and teaching reveals that there are very few studies, particularly in its application to HE. The Manchester Metropolitan sub-project centres on one of the applications of transmedia

---

5. https://transmedialiteracy.org

storytelling in language education. The main goal of the *New Approaches to Transmedia and Language Pedagogy* project is

> "to bridge the gap between transmedia and L2 studies, both in secondary and higher education[6]. [It] has several interrelated objectives: 1. exploring the digital, media and visual skills of the Millennial and Generation Z and their cultures; 2. examining how transmedia projects can provide opportunities to supplement or complement traditional modes of L2 learning and teaching, and assessment; 3. testing new learning scenarios that allow for the development of innovative student-centred educational practices, and the implementation of collaborative strategies that ultimately meet the 21st century students' needs and future job skills and profiles [engaging students in critically reading and composing multimodal texts]" (Transmedia in education, n.p.[7]).

From an interdisciplinary perspective, introducing projects based on films and video-games allows students to engage critically and creatively with some of the most popular forms of media entertainment in the world and to explore a wide range of multimodal resources (animation, image, sound, music, text, etc.). Language learners can also reflect analytically on their work and their engagement with different transmedia concepts (narrative functions, prosumer, interaction, remix, narrativity, among others). The implementation of these projects and assessment of these skills can be done via wikis (in Moodle/Blackboard platforms) and videos (via the university YouTube channel), both as objects of self-assessment and peer assessment[8]. The ultimate goal is to design a framework for introducing video games and transmedia practices in the language classroom based on research and practices. As a part of the project,

---

6. Transmedia storytelling, that involves expressing messages and stories across the media spectrum (films and television series, social media, books, video games...) and making use of the affordances offered in each media channel, offers creative opportunities in four areas (Jenkins et al., 2009): backstory, mapping the world, displaying other character's perspectives on the action, and expanding audience engagement.

7. http://transmediaineducation.com/

8. An example of the implementation of these principles and activities can be seen in the The FaCE Project (Film and Creative Engagement) https://bit.ly/2RZSTeL

researchers have created resources that have been piloted in an INSET. The resources are also available in the project website (for French and Spanish). These resources will be complemented with a teachers' toolkit that will be published in 2019. The final phase of this project comprises of a symposium and an international conference, which will take place in Manchester in April and June 2019.

3. Conclusion

Under the impact of technology, the prevalence of media and visual forms of communication stresses the need for engaging students in critically reading and composing multimodal texts. Given the explosion of user-generated content online (Wikipedia, Facebook, YouTube, blogs, and multimedia message services), it is quite apparent that language curricula should take into account the current prosumer (producer and consumer) profile and abilities of the young networked generation (under 30's).

Furthermore, over the past decade, the relevance of visual cultures has been growing. Different streaming services such as Apple, Amazon, HBO, Netflix, and particularly YouTube are shaping how we consume, interact, and communicate with media. The engagement with media in a multi-screen, multi-platform, multilingual networked digital environment is a trend particularly relevant to media and cultural studies, but also to the field of language studies as contemporary visual and transmedia culture is fundamentally transnational and *glocal*. Acknowledging all these trends, the *New Approaches to Transmedia and Language Pedagogy* project aims to exploit the opportunities and affordances in this media landscape. It offers teacher training and research-based strategies and activities suitable for supporting the development of transmedia literacy, which implies the ability to recognise, understand, and interact with complex, multimodal narratives. At the same time, it aims to foster the development of intercultural awareness and critical thinking and broaden other competences (e.g. translingual, transcultural, creativity, digital, and transmedia skills).

Acknowledgements

This work was supported by the UK Arts and Humanities Research Council's Open World Research Initiative (OWRI, https://ahrc.ukri.org/research/funded themesandprogrammes/themes/owri/), under the programme 'Cross-Language Dynamics: Reshaping Community', and the Manchester Metropolitan University.

References

Bakhshi, H., Downing, J., Osborne, M., & Schneider, P. (2017). *The future of skills: employment in 2030*. Pearson and Nesta. https://www.pearson.com/corporate/about-pearson/innovation/future-obs.html

British Academy. (2016). *Born Global. A British Academy project on languages and employability.* http://www.britac.ac.uk/born-global

Chan, D., & Herrero, C. (2010). *Using film to teach languages.* Manchester, Routes into Languages, the UK Film Council and Cornerhouse. https://goo.gl/oP4t3A

Domínguez Romero, E., Bobkina, J., & Stefanova, S. (Eds). (2018). *Teaching literature and language through multimodal texts.* IGI Global.

Forsdick, C. (2017). Age cannot wither her, nor custom stale her infinite variety. In *Do we need modern language graduates in a globalised world?* The Times Higher Education. https://www.timeshighereducation.com/features/do-we-need-modern-language-graduates-in-globalised-world

Gramling, D. (2017). The devil can cite Scripture for his purpose. In *Do we need modern language graduates in a globalised world?* The Times Higher Education. https://www.timeshighereducation.com/features/do-we-need-modern-language-graduates-in-globalised-world

Herrero, C. (2019). Medios audiovisuales (audiovisual media). In J. Muñoz-Basols, E. Gironzetti & M. Lacorte (Eds), *The Routledge handbook of Spanish language teaching: metodologías, contextos y recursos para la enseñanza del español L2* (pp. 565-582). Routledge.

Herrero, C., & Vanderschelden, I. (Eds). (2019). *Using film and media in the language classroom: reflections on research-led teaching.* Multilingual Matters.

Jenkins, H. (2006). *Convergence culture: where old and new media collide.* NYU press.

Jenkins, H., Purushotma, R., Weigel, M., Clinton, K., & Robison, A. J. (2009). *Confronting the challenges of participatory culture. media education for the 21st century.* The MIT Press. https://doi.org/10.7551/mitpress/8435.001.0001

Kalantzis, M., Cope, B., Chan, E., & Dalley-Trim, L. (2015). *Literacies*. Cambridge University Press.

Kelly, M. (2017). True is it that we have seen better days. In *Do we need modern language graduates in a globalised world?* The Times Higher Education. https://www.timeshighereducation.com/features/do-we-need-modern-language-graduates-in-globalised-world

Kern, R. (2003). Literacy as a new organizing principle for foreign language education. In P. C. Patrikis (Ed.), *Reading between the lines: perspectives on foreign language literacy* (pp. 40-59). Yale University Press.

Kress, G., & van Leeuwen, L. (2001). *Multimodal discourses: modes and media of contemporary communication*. Oxford University Press.

Paesani, K., Allen, H. W., & Dupuy, B. (2016). *A multiliteracies framework for collegiate foreign language teaching*. Pearson.

Scolari, C. (2018). *Transmedia literacy in the new media ecology: white paper*. Universitat Pompey Fabra. Department de comunicació.

Verstraete-Hansen, L. (2017). Something is rotten in the state of Denmark. In *Do we need modern language graduates in a globalised world?* The Times Higher Education. https://www.timeshighereducation.com/features/do-we-need-modern-language-graduates-in-globalised-world

Section 2.

Active learning and student empowerment

4. Supporting and empowering language teachers through action research communities

Angela Gallagher-Brett[1]

Abstract

This chapter will introduce Action Research Communities for Language Teachers (ARC), a project funded by the European Centre for Modern Languages (ECML) of the Council of Europe (2015-2018). The project aims to make action research techniques widely available to language teachers across Europe and to provide them with development opportunities which support them in conducting action research. The chapter provides an overview of the project and the training and development events organised, and highlights examples of action research projects undertaken by participating practitioners in schools and universities. It concludes with details of challenges and successes experienced by participants, and considerations of future steps.

Keywords: action research, professional development, language teaching, collaboration.

1. Introduction

ARC is a project funded by the ECML of the Council of Europe. The project aims to raise the profile of action research for language teachers across Europe

---

1. SOAS, University of London, London, England; ag62@soas.ac.uk

How to cite this chapter: Gallagher-Brett, A. (2019). Supporting and empowering language teachers through action research communities. In N. Becerra, R. Biasini, H. Magedera-Hofhansl & A. Reimão (Eds), *Innovative language teaching and learning at university: a look at new trends* (pp. 29-36). Research-publishing.net. https://doi.org/10.14705/rpnet.2019.32.899

and to show how undertaking action research can both empower teachers and benefit learners. This is being achieved by making techniques for action research widely available to language teachers; strengthening professional networks by linking academic expertise on action research and good practice in language classrooms and by enabling teachers to reflect on practice and to test innovations within a community of practice (Gallagher-Brett & Lechner, 2017). Within these broader aims, the ARC team has also set out to design action research tools to support teachers in different educational sectors in conducting their own action research and to create European models for peer learning.

Action research puts teachers at the centre of creating educational change and developing increased knowledge and understanding of their own practice (Elliott, 1991, 2011). It starts from practical questions that teachers may have about their teaching and offers them a range of research tools and techniques that they can employ to investigate these questions, including research journals, observations, interviews, photography, video recordings, and dossiers (Feldman, Altrichter, Posch, & Somekh, 2018).

Action research involves a continual cycle of action and reflection and has the potential to empower teachers to act autonomously in their own classrooms and to bring about improvements to teaching (e.g. Altrichter & Posch, 2007; Elliott, 2011). It also supports them in developing the skills of systematic inquiry into their own practice (Kemmis & McTaggart, 1982). The ARC team therefore considers that action research is a significant professional development tool for language teachers. Its collaborative nature also means that it can help teachers feel less isolated (Burns, 2005), which we propose could be important for language teachers who often work as individuals, sometimes as the only language teacher in a school (Borthwick & Gallagher-Brett, 2014).

In this paper, I provide an overview of the project, which is a work in progress, and the training and development opportunities organised by the ARC team. My focus is on outputs from the main project workshop held in Graz in November 2016. I also highlight examples of action research projects undertaken by participants and discuss project challenges and successes.

2. Method

As one of the central aims of the ARC project has been to encourage classroom practitioners with differing levels of expertise to engage with action research, we were particularly keen to adopt a practical approach and therefore utilised Altrichter and Posch (2007). We believed that this accessible text, which is also available in English (e.g. Feldman et al., 2018) would be helpful to teachers as it can support them in carrying out and reporting on classroom projects. It provides detailed practical guidance on finding starting points for research, formulating research plans, collecting and analysing data, developing action strategies, and making practitioners' knowledge public.

We began by organising a series of conversations between partners with the aim of bringing together our diverse European action research traditions and ensuring that these were included in our approach. We then conducted discussions with language teachers in different educational sectors to obtain a range of perspectives on action research and on the likely training and development needs of teachers interested in carrying out this approach. We held action research workshops for teachers in different European countries where they were introduced to action research tools and techniques and invited to explore aspects of interest in their own practice and to develop collaborative plans for projects. Key project events held to date are listed in Table 1.

Table 1. Key professional development events organised by ARC

Event	Participants	Event aims
April 2016: International Week Pedagogical University Tirol, Austria	Higher education language teacher educators and pre-service teachers	• Discussions on quality and enhancement in language teaching at tertiary level across Europe and on the role of action research in enhancing quality
October 2016: Action research CPD workshop in Sibiu/Hermannstadt, Romania	German teachers from different educational sectors	• Introduction to action research tools and techniques • Discussions on finding a starting point in investigating classroom practice • Planning collaborative action research projects

Chapter 4

November 2016: Main project CPD workshop at ECML, Graz, Austria	Language teachers from different sectors, teacher educators, language advisory teachers	• Introduction to action research tools and techniques • Discussions on finding a starting point in investigating classroom practice • Planning collaborative projects
May 2018: Action research network meeting at ECML, Graz, Austria	Selection of language teachers from previous Graz workshop	• Presentation of action research projects undertaken and feedback
June 2018: Action research CPD workshop Reykjavik, Iceland	Language teachers from different educational sectors	• Introduction to action research tools and techniques • Discussions on finding a starting point in investigating classroom practice • Planning collaborative action research projects

Our main project workshop in Graz in November 2016 attracted school and university language teachers and teacher educators from 31 European countries. Participants were invited to present on an aspect of language teaching practice in their own contexts and to gain a deeper understanding of the issues involved using the methodology of analytic discourse. We also introduced action research methods and the concept of action research cycles (Altrichter & Posch, 2007). Participants then formed into groups with those of similar interests or contexts and developed plans for small collaborative classroom projects. They subsequently returned home to begin work on their projects and members of the ARC team acted as critical friends, providing advice and feedback during the process in line with Stenhouse's (1975) ideas (as cited in Kember et al., 1997). Initial results were reported in either English or German and were shared with the wider project community via Padlet. Participants were then invited to present their findings and to discuss next steps for their research at a network meeting in Graz in May 2018.

3. Results and discussion

The main project workshop in Graz resulted in project plans spanning a wide range of topics and interests including critical thinking (involving participants from Albania, Latvia, Netherlands, Malta), the use of social media in language teaching (Iceland, Croatia), and teachers as co-constructors of knowledge (Bulgaria, Germany, Norway, Slovenia, Switzerland) among others. Several projects included cross-sector partnerships involving school and university teachers and almost all included collaboration between teachers in different countries. The only exception to this was a project on teaching vocabulary strategies in Ireland which involved participants from different sectors – English as an Additional Language (EAL) and primary Modern Foreign Languages (MFL) – working together.

Although a small number of participants withdrew from engagement, ten of eleven proposed projects were completed, which seemed to us to demonstrate a high level of engagement with the process. Examples from completed projects are described below.

Participants from Finland and France investigated the role of a range of student-centred activities in the language classroom among university learners of German (Finland) and English (France). They found that students were very motivated by these activities but that they needed to be carefully planned and scaffolded. They concluded that action research is an effective means of supporting teachers' professional development (Maijala & Pagèze, 2018). In Ireland, our participants trained EAL and MFL teachers to teach vocabulary-noticing strategies. On their return to school, the teachers trained learners in language support and MFL classes in using the strategies. Data collected from students by means of questionnaires showed that they felt better able to cope with learning after being introduced to the strategies. Questionnaires and interviews with teachers revealed that they found the experience of doing action research empowering, (Kenny & Puig, 2018) in line with suggestions in the literature (Elliott, 2011). In Serbia and the Former Yugoslav Republic of Macedonia, research was conducted by our participants into the attitudinal and motivational impact of embracing Content and Language Integrated Learning (CLIL) as a teaching methodology in vocational schools. Using student questionnaires and interviews, Manic and Gjoreska (2018) found that students reported greater confidence and enjoyment from attending CLIL classes than standard language classes.

Chapter 4

There were challenges along the way both during the professional development events and in participants' project outputs. As members of the ARC team, we found it difficult to cover all the required ground on action research methods in our workshops and had to improvise and provide additional advice to teachers once their action research was underway.

Several of the proposed collaborations did not work effectively and teachers reported instances of co-collaborators agreeing to do the action research, but then finding themselves unable to commit to it or find the time.

As we expected, university participants were more familiar with conducting and writing up research than school teachers. A group of four school teachers from the main Graz workshop in 2016 experienced difficulties in following the action research cycle and in reporting on their research. It became clear when they presented their findings at our network meeting in May 2018 that they had carried out investigations into aspects of lesson planning using research tools, which they had found valuable but that their reports did not constitute action research. The ARC team therefore subsequently devised a checklist of detailed steps in the action research cycle to enable these teachers to move on from their exploratory results and to report more explicitly on the different stages of their action research. Two of these teachers have succeeded in doing that and we are hopeful that the others will complete their research successfully.

4. Conclusions

Overall, we believe that the ability of participants to conduct and complete their projects has been successful, as evidenced in the high levels of engagement and project completion. Examples highlighted show that action research has supported professional development and has empowered teachers. We are also gathering feedback on the impact of the broader community of practice as participants have reported that they gained encouragement from each other and from the ARC team.

We are continuing to work with participants to finalise their results and to explore with them the next steps in their action research journeys. This remains ongoing work. Whilst we are greatly encouraged by the successes experienced, it remains to be seen whether teachers will continue with action research once the project is over.

The ARC team is also working on an annotated action research spiral which can be used as a tool for language teachers who would like to do action research and on open resources for action research. All project results and resources will be shared on the website (www.ecml/at/actionresearch) and it is hoped that these will be useful for teachers from across Europe.

Acknowledgements

I would like to thank the ECML and ARC project partners: Christine Lechner (Pedagogical University Tirol), Tita Mihaiu (Centrul pentru formarea continuă în limba germană, CPD), Brynhildur Ragnarsdóttir (Language Centre, Reykjavik), Renata Zanin (University of Bolzano-Bozen), Marianne Jacquin (University of Geneva), Jim Murphy (Centre for Distance Learning and Innovation, Canada), and Melanie Steiner and Anita Konrad (Pedagogical University Tirol).

I would also extend my thanks to the project participants: Minna Maijala (University of Turku), Joanne Pagèze (University of Bordeaux), Mary Kenny (ESOL Development Officer, Dublin, and Dun Laoghaire ETB), and Kenia Puig (Post-Primary MFL Initiative, Ireland).

References

Altrichter, H., & Posch, P. (2007) *LehrerInnen und Lehrer erforschen ihren Unterricht. Unterrichtsentwicklung und Unterrichtsevaluation durch Aktionforschung* (4th ed.). Klinkhardt.

Borthwick, K., & Gallagher-Brett, A. (2014). 'Inspiration, ideas, encouragement': teacher development and improved use of technology in language teaching through open educational practice. *Computer Assisted Language Learning, 27*(2), 163-183. https://doi.org/10.1080/09588221.2013.818560

Burns, A. (2005). Action research: an evolving paradigm. *Language Teaching, 38*(2), 57-74. https://doi.org/10.1017/S0261444805002661

Elliott, J. (1991). *Action research for educational change.* Open University Press.

Elliott, J. (2011). *The educational action research and the teacher.* http://www.actionresearch.gr/AR/ActionResearch_Vol1/Issue01_01_p01-03.pdf

Feldman, A., Altrichter, H., Posch, P., & Somekh, B. (2018). *Teachers investigate their work: an introduction to action research across the professions* (3rd ed.). Routledge.

Gallagher-Brett, A., & Lechner, C. (2017). Enhancing language teaching through action research for language teachers. *In Reflecting on action research in an unequal world: an alternative perspective towards democracy, CARN Annual Conference, 20-22 October 2017, University of Crete, Rethymno, Greece.*

Kember, D., Ha, T. S., Lam, B. H., Lee, A., Yan, L., & Yum, J. (1997). The diverse role of the critical friend in supporting educational action research projects. *Educational Action Research, 5*(3), 463-481. https://doi.org/10.1080/09650799700200036

Kemmis, S., & McTaggart, R. (1982). *The action research planner.* Deakin University Press.

Kenny, M., & Puig, K. (2018). *Does teaching vocabulary noticing strategies lead to learner autonomy?* Report for Action Research Communities for Language Teachers, ECML. https://www.ecml.at/ECML-Programme/Programme2016-2019/Professionallearningcommunities/Successstories/tabid/4143/language/en-GB/Default.aspx

Maijala, M., & Pagèze, J. (2018). *How do different types of student-centred activities function in the FL classroom?* Report for Action Research Communities for Language Teachers, ECML. https://www.ecml.at/ECML-Programme/Programme2016-2019/Professionallearningcommunities/Successstories/tabid/4143/language/en-GB/Default.aspx

Manic, D. & Gjoreska, D. (2018). *CLIL in secondary vocational schools seen through the students' perspectives.* Report for Action Research Communities for Language Teachers, ECML. https://www.ecml.at/ECML-Programme/Programme2016-2019/Professionallearningcommunities/Successstories/tabid/4143/language/en-GB/Default.aspx

Stenhouse, L. (1975). *An introduction to curriculum research and development.* Heinemann.

5. Independent reading together – combining self-directed and collaborative learning

Theresa Federici[1]

Abstract

This paper proposes a way of integrating self-directed reading into a collaborative classroom with formative and summative tasks as well as facilitating integration with the target culture, and familiarity with the target language in a variety of settings. Linking to literature on motivation, and drawing on case-study experience, an approach to introducing students to reading for pleasure in the target language will be suggested. The core element of the project is complete freedom of choice for students in the book they select, enabling students to match their personal reading tastes to their target language reading. Students benefit from the selection process and from discussion and comparison with peers on the selected texts. Students' awareness of forms of literature in the target language is enriched through the diversity of texts chosen within the cohort.

Keywords: literature, critical skills, learner-autonomy, motivation.

1. Introduction

This paper describes a project that brought self-directed independent Target Language (TL) reading into a communicative language classroom. The project was integrated into a language module for second year (advanced) undergraduate students of Italian. However, it could be adapted for final year undergraduates

---

1. Cardiff University, Cardiff, Wales; federici:@cardiff.ac.uk; https://orcid.org/0000-0002-9875-7583

How to cite this chapter: Federici, T. (2019) Independent reading together – combining self-directed and collaborative learning. In N. Becerra, R. Biasini, H. Magedera-Hofhansl & A. Reimão (Eds), *Innovative language teaching and learning at university: a look at new trends* (pp. 37-44). Research-publishing.net. https://doi.org/10.14705/rpnet.2019.32.900

and for different languages. In this case, out of the three weekly contact hours, one hour was dedicated to independent reading. The reading element ran for one semester (ten hours); but would be well-suited to running across two semesters.

The purpose of the reading element was to equip students with the information and autonomy to select a book that appeals to their individual taste, and to share this with peers. No limitations were placed on book selection; students were free to choose from fiction or non-fiction. I intended to address two issues: (1) student engagement, and (2) integration and motivation. Firstly, when language modules include set-reading, student performance and engagement could considerably vary based on students' opinions of the book. I wanted to understand whether students' views were based on language comprehension or on content, and whether, if students were able to choose their own reading material, they would perceive the comprehension difficulties in the same way. Secondly, students were provided with the competences to choose their own reading material to facilitate their integration into the TL culture during their year abroad. Integrative motivation is a crucial component in L2 acquisition, as many studies have illustrated (Coleman, 1996; Dörnyei & Csizér, 2002; Ushioda, 2001), and language courses are an ideal environment for students to further explore TL culture in a more personalised way.

This paper provides an overview of the considerations underpinning my materials design, and an outline of the structure of the reading project as I implemented it. It concludes with some findings from the perspective of the tutor and the learner.

2. Method

2.1. Materials design considerations

2.1.1. Managing academic requirements

As students have many academic pressures, reading for pleasure may not be a priority. Adopting a process-led approach (see White & Arndt, 1991) enabled students to articulate their opinions alongside their independent reading. The act of reading became intrinsic and relevant to the class activities. Students were able to compare and contrast authors and writing strategies. Ambition and expectation need careful management: students were made aware of the time available and of the summative review-writing task. By integrating a reading element in a manageable way within the course and having regular formative and summative outcomes, I hoped to give students the space to explore TL literature.

2.1.2. Managing student expectations

As individual choice was fundamental to the aims of greater TL autonomy and confidence, no boundaries were placed on genre. In an earlier version of this course I experimented with selecting the genre of detective fiction. I decided not to repeat this as students commented that having a set text would be as limiting as choosing a book from a genre they did not like. I thought I was providing a safer environment by limiting choice, but students' feedback differed – and was immensely valuable. In this revised approach, the only limitation was that students chose something they would read for pleasure. I nonetheless needed to support students and advise on the suitability of books (length, dialect) to avoid disappointment or demotivation. Choices included historical novels, fan-fiction, biographies, and teen-novels. Some chose two books, either rejecting their first choice, or because they wanted to read both. This process of discovery furthers the development of students' TL ideal-self identity (Hadfield & Dörnyei, 2013), and empowers students to see a place for themselves within the TL culture, to encounter like-minded groups: to find their TL 'niche'.

2.1.3. Managing the group dynamic

Each student has different motivations, interests, and influences creating their TL identity. Freedom of choice in reading is aligned with Williams and Burden's (1997) social constructivist model of learner individuality and a dynamic learning environment in which tasks are interpreted "in ways that are meaningful and personal" (p. 43). It was hoped to create a meaningful and *personal* context, that would lead to a number of *co-operative* tasks, in which individuality would lead to a collaborative and supportive group dynamic. Group dynamics can influence students' self-perceptions both positively and negatively (Ushioda, 2003), and group norms vary greatly depending on group composition. I was keen to see the effect of individual book choices on the dynamic, particularly in groups with wide-ranging language abilities. When students compete and compare, destructive norms may ensue, such as over-reliance on stronger students, or reticence in participating: such phenomena were diminished through individual book choices. There was genuine interest in peers' choices and views, thus fulfilling Hadfield's (1992) key elements of successful group processes, including support, co-operation, and empathy (mentioned in Williams & Burden, 1997, p. 195).

2.2. Structuring the reading element

2.2.1. Supporting learners in their choices

Students needed to be primed for the notion of choosing their own TL book to read for pleasure as this was an unknown experience for many students. Asking directly which books or authors students like can create a negative response, raised affective filters, and a lack of engagement. Using online quizzes from TL newspapers, social media, or magazines was a good entry into debate, as was talking about children's literature. TL book seller websites are also a good source of information as some include lists of best sellers or Top 10 by genre. Bringing a variety of TL novels the tutor owns to the class can also be very interesting; students enjoy the tactile experience of examining the covers and flipping through the pages. In fact, asking students to 'judge a book by its cover' is a stimulating activity that increases exposure to TL literature. Reviews and book 'blurbs' then followed, as students began to narrow down their options and make their choice of novel.

Students consolidate a range of autonomous skills in the TL. They are independently *navigating* and *reading* TL media and reviews with a clear and genuine purpose: to select their book of choice. These activities increase student confidence in their own abilities and also facilitate exposure to the TL culture. Students reported that they had asked TL friends and acquaintances for recommendations, thus purposefully using TL for spoken and written communication. The 'academic' outcome of identifying and selecting a TL book is far exceeded by the *process* involved in arriving at a choice of book, in terms of TL exposure, confidence at engaging with TL environments, and language acquisition. This engagement with TL sources is a means to an end, a necessary step to choose a book, hence students do not focus on the quantity of TL exposure they gain. In comparison to courses with a set text, the process of selecting a book offers students significant opportunities for independent and purposeful interaction and engagement with the TL.

2.2.2. Scaffolding the reading process

The absence of a set-text demands a clear structure for classes in which students commented on their own reading process. These classes engaged with different writing techniques including narrative voice, creation of characters, use of language, and descriptive language. This facilitated comparative discussions amongst students on their own books. Communication became purposeful as students advocated for their chosen author. The process involved is again multi-faceted: awareness of TL discourse analysis is increased through collaborative discussions. Collaborative writing enabled students to work together on accuracy, lexical choices, and persuasive writing. Peer review was embedded into these activities with groups reading each other's written work. Students could have fun with these in-class activities, lowering affective filters (Krashen, 1981). The social dimension helps create purpose for writing, and the peer-reviewing increases awareness of readership, which in turn supports accurate communication.

A supportive and collaborative environment was enhanced by individual book choices: students' awareness of TL authors broadened as recommendations were made among students. Students were genuinely interested in each other's choices, and peer-engagement became an important vehicle for increased and continued reading for pleasure in the TL.

Chapter 5

2.2.3. Creating assessment with a genuine purpose

From the outset, students knew their summative task would be loading their own book review onto an Italian website. This review became one of the standardised summative tasks for language modules, which was a short written task (+/- 300 words). Introducing authentic assessment, the 'publishing' of their review written in the TL on a website, enabled students to self-reflect. Just as they had read reviews to select their book, now they were completing this cycle by adding their own review to the same website, which may then influence others – even native speakers – when considering that book.

The authentic task enabled learners to consider a genuine readership, and to create the content of their review as a purposeful act of genuine communication. The review contained their personal perspectives, there were no right or wrong answers in terms of opinion; students could hate the book without fear of their summative mark being affected. In the written and verbal feedback, I commented on the persuasiveness of their review. Maintaining authenticity allowed me to assess purposeful communication through the rigours of the established marking criteria for the degree programme – as any summative task would be. Each assessment was unique, a snapshot of an individual's experience and perception of the book that they read.

3. Results and discussion

3.1. Student perspective

In the case study group most had only read TL books that were part of an educational programme (school/degree) and independently interacting with TL media was a new but empowering experience. Through weekly writing tasks I could assess language progression. Over the duration of the project, written work became more confident, accurate, and succinct, although causality of these improvements would be difficult to isolate. I could ascertain students' development in critical awareness through in-class activities based on their opinions of their author. Peer-communication became purposeful as students became advocates for their choice of novel. Initially, some students were concerned about reading a complete book, however, they ultimately experienced a sense of achievement and pride in reading their 'own' book. Some did not manage to finish within the semester, however, they commented that completion of the book had become a personal challenge. Autonomy and freedom of choice empowered students to engage with their text beyond the classroom environment.

3.2. Tutor perspective

Unlike reading a set-text with which students are (literally) on the same page, and are asked to progress at the same speed, the focus here significantly shifts from the tutor as leader, guiding the reading, to students being the 'authority' on their individual book, but with a clear structure of classroom activities to enable individual and collaborative learning. The tutor maintains responsibility for guiding acquisition of language skills – what changes is the subject-matter each student brings, not the associated language skills. This change in dynamic with the tutor not having all the answers in terms of critical reading, leads to more genuine interaction patterns. In this case study, this dynamic added enthusiasm and increased participation, and interactions were found to be more spontaneous and engaged.

4. Conclusions

The benefits of this approach were articulated by students in class-based activities. They were aware of their increased TL competences, particularly in acquisition of vocabulary, both from their own reading and from finding out about the texts chosen by others. The process-led dynamic and pedagogical framework enabled students to personalise learning and gain a sense of TL integration. This approach does not replace set-texts, but by interspersing set-text reading and free choice reading, students' competences, confidence, and cultural awareness can be enriched throughout their degree course.

References

Coleman, J. A. (1996). *Studying languages*. CILT.

Dörnyei, Z., & Csizér, K. (2002). Some dynamics of language attitudes and motivations. *Applied Linguistics, 23*(4), 421-462. https://doi.org/10.1093/applin/23.4.421

Hadfield. J. (1992). *Classroom dynamics*. Oxford University Press.

Hadfield, J., & Dörnyei, Z. (2013). *Motivating learning*. Routledge.

Krashen, S. D. (1981). *Second language acquisition and second language learning*. Pergamon Press.

Ushioda, E. (2001). Language learning at university: exploring the role of motivational thinking. In Z. Dörnyei & R. Schmidt (Eds), *Motivation and second language acquisition* (pp. 93-125). University of Hawaii.

Ushioda, E. (2003). Motivation as a socially mediated process. In D. Little, J. Ridley & E. Ushioda (Eds), *Learner autonomy in the foreign language classroom: teacher, learner, curriculum and assessment* (pp. 90-102). Authentik.

White, R., & Arndt, V. (1991). *Process writing*. Longman.

Williams, M., & Burden, R. L. (1997). *Psychology for language teachers: a social constructivist approach*. Cambridge University Press.

6 Process drama and theatre in the learning of Italian. The case of 'I Promessi sposi di Birmingham, un "romanzo criminale"'

Fabrizio Di Maio[1]

Abstract

This paper illustrates the use of two language-teaching and learning methods (process drama and theatre) in a class of Italian. Process drama is based on improvisation, over-identification, and dramatisation from a short set of coordinates that students can read just a few minutes before the activity that will be later performed in class (see Dunn, 2016; Giebert, 2014; Hulse & Owens, 2017; Jun, 2001; Kao & O'Neill, 1998; O'Neill, 1995; Piazzoli, 2010; Pirola, 2011). Theatre, on the contrary, is based on a script; it involves actors, a director, costumes, set, props, and an audience (see, Fonio, 2012; Guerra & Militello, 2011; Marini-Maio & Ryan-Scheutz, 2010). These methods promote different learning experiences and through reflection on my teaching experience I demonstrate how both process drama and theatre can enrich the student experience and foster a creative and imaginative use of the foreign language in and outside the classroom.

Keywords: process drama, theatre, engagement, learning by doing.

---

1. Teaching Fellow, University of Birmingham, Birmingham, England; f.dimaio@bham.ac.uk

How to cite this chapter: Di Maio, F. (2019). Process drama and theatre in the learning of Italian. The case of 'I Promessi sposi di Birmingham, un "romanzo criminale"'. In N. Becerra, R. Biasini, H. Magedera-Hofhansl & A. Reimão (Eds), *Innovative language teaching and learning at university: a look at new trends* (pp. 45-51). Research-publishing.net. https://doi.org/10.14705/rpnet.2019.32.901

Chapter 6

1. Introduction

This paper describes activities from two language-learning methods, process drama and theatre, conducted with first year advanced students of Italian. In process drama, students experience an event through improvisation rather than rehearsing or presenting a final performance (Hulse & Owens, 2017). At the beginning of the class, students receive a short text in which the initial moments of a situation along with location and roles are presented. After having taken their roles, students will improvise the developments of the events (Piazzoli, 2010; Pirola, 2011). For a positive outcome of the process drama, the tutor needs to determine the context on which the instructions will be based, taking into account the learners' linguistic abilities, sociocultural backgrounds, and skills.

In addition, theatre, intended as a didactic method, contemplates a script, students/ actors who rehearse their roles, a tutor/director who instructs the actors, along with an environment created concretely through costumes, make-up, scenery, and props (Marini-Maio & Ryan-Scheutz, 2010; Ryan-Scheutz & Colangelo, 2004,). Staging a play is very useful for foreign language students as they can at once enhance their linguistic, sociolinguistic, and pragmatic competences, as well as enjoy an intercultural experience (Fonio, 2012).

2. Method

In 2017-2018, in the first semester, I worked with six first-year advanced students – across two oral hours over two terms of ten weeks each – on process drama activities[2]. At the beginning of every class, students received a set of instructions on which the outcome is always unpredictable, leaving them free to imagine and invent any possible development[3]. Most importantly, as they

---

2. The Core Module is structured in six weekly teaching hours: one hour lecture, one hour seminar, two hour analytical skills (based on a grammar book), and two hour communicative skills (based on process drama and theatre).

3. Topics of pre-texts used include: dinner invitation; murder in the university; probable suicide; marriage proposal with misunderstanding; lies or truths; problems in holidays; cheating on your partner; wrong booking; and mad scientist who switches brains (see supplementary materials, Part 1 for an example; https://research-publishing.box.com/s/n7d27peyclx74bf1hofzfzjx51lxqllu).

do not have time to rehearse, language is used in a spontaneous way (O'Neill, 1995; Piazzoli, 2010). Like in real life circumstances, speakers need to cope with unpredictable developments of events and consequently students are pushed to use the language effectively with the resources they possess. The benefits of improvised dramatic activities are particularly relevant to the unpredictability of language, which is by its very nature unplanned, and every statement is open to any response (Hulse & Owens, 2017).

Based on improvisation and dramatisation (Hulse & Owens, 2017; Pirola, 2011), the other essential trait of process drama is that it is not intended for any audience (DICE, 2010), except students and tutor. In this way, students feel more relaxed in class during the activities

Indeed, process drama helps "to bridge the gap between the [safe] and controlled world of the classroom and the seemingly chaotic composition of language in the [outside] world" (Dougill, 1987 cited in Carson, 2012, p. 51). Therefore, students are able to practise the language and the appropriate behaviour to complex situations in the safety of the classroom, where drama activities lower affective barriers and enhance the benefits of a collaborative task (Giebert, 2014).

I implemented the use of process drama in the first semester to offer the students the possibility of being more creative in their use of Italian. At the end of the semester, the students were enthusiastic about process drama because it helped them improve their confidence as well as their linguistic skills, especially fluency, pronunciation, and vocabulary. Process drama was also very successful as it promoted students' active and central role in the learning experience.

At the beginning of the second term, we moved from process drama to theatre in order to enhance other language competences, i.e. writing an original script in a foreign language. Taking inspiration from Alessandro Manzoni's *I promessi sposi* (*The Betrothed*, 1827-1840), a set text in the core module, students rewrote the characters of the novel, changing the essence of the characters as well as the city where the story was set.

In the first part of the class, students wrote cooperatively an original script using Google Docs, while in the second part they performed the scenes. My role was to facilitate their work, giving advice on the development of the plot and then on the performance. In particular, I checked the linguistic accuracy, leaving the structure and the content of the plot to the students[4]. During the performance, I gave them suggestions on acting – based on my previous experiences and studies in theatre – specifically on body language and pronunciation.

As shown in end of semester questionnaires, students enjoyed the classes because they had the chance to put into practice skills such writing, speaking, and performing in Italian[5]. Every week, students had sufficient time to rethink the evolution of their characters, along with the development of the plot, actions, and dialogues.

At the end of the module, students wrote an original script that completely transformed the original plot. *I promessi sposi*, set in Lombardy at the beginning of the 17th century, is now located in 2018 Birmingham: *I promessi sposi di Birmingham, "un romanzo criminale"* [The Betrothed of Birmingham, "a Criminal Story"][6]. The main characters Don Rodrigo and Renzo are now two drug dealers who fight to have control of the city. The events and dialogues reveal a world dominated by drug trafficking, kidnappings, betrayals, and murderers.

These teaching methods have been reflected in the assessment. The oral assessment (for process drama) took place at the end of the first semester in the following format: on the day of the exam, students received relevant coordinates (i.e. indications of roles and events that they had to develop through improvisation). In pairs, they had 20 minutes to prepare before the exam. They were assessed on correctness/appropriateness of language used, intonation/

---

4. Students and tutor shared the same document. Therefore, I could check what they were writing.

5. The module questionnaire given at the end of the first semester included questions such as: 'Did process drama enhance your speaking skills?', 'Were the activities challenging?', 'What did you enjoy the most?', 'How can the activities be improved?'. Students' comments were extremely positive, and their appreciation was expressed in both informal comments and in the module questionnaires.

6. See supplementary materials, Part 2; https://research-publishing.box.com/s/n7d27peyclx74bf1hofzfzjx511xqllu

pronunciation, and listening/comprehension. These competences have been introduced on a weekly basis, so the students were able to concentrate not only on the fluency of their communication, but also on language accuracy.

The oral exam (for theatre) took place at the end of the second semester and was divided in two parts. First, the performance (30 minutes, 50% of the mark) with the focus on the following criteria: body language, pronunciation/intonation, and communicative competence. Students worked on these competences during the semester. The second consisted of an interview (about ten minutes for each student, 50% of the mark) with three additional criteria: accuracy, range of structures, and development of ideas. In the interview, the tutor was a journalist/interviewer and the students were the actors who played the roles.

3. Results and discussion

Regarding process drama, students enjoyed the fact that it was presented as a different pedagogical method to those used in other language modules. In particular, students seemed very at ease (regardless of their competence in the language) to step into uncertain situations only knowing the starting point. Indeed, "effective language learning requires opportunities for authentic verbal interactions" (Hulse & Owens, 2017, p. 18; see also Kao & O'Neill, 1998). These interactions let students produce language in a more practical way and consequently pass from familiar to unfamiliar contexts without excessive anxiety (Hulse & Owens, 2017). As process drama is an open-ended activity, students were the protagonists and actively decided how the stories would develop.

Even if theatre does not share many of the aspects related to process drama (i.e. improvisation, no script, open-ended stories), students participated with passion in the creation of an original script and were able to enhance their writing skills by inventing a story and helping each other to give the characters a similar amount of space and dialogue in the plot. During the rehearsals, students improved their speaking skills through practise, with special attention to pronunciation, intonation, and accuracy.

4. Conclusions

Although, as shown, process drama and theatre have different features, students can directly apply the classic concept of 'learning by doing' (Dewey, 1938) in both methods. Referring to the above-mentioned experiences, the way of learning through process drama and theatre is highly motivating for students and gives them the opportunity to experience a foreign language in a collaborative and engaging context. This aspect of the learning experience is not to be overlooked: university students are exposed to a lot of pressure and stress since they have to deal with assignments and exams throughout the academic year. Process drama and theatre activities, on the contrary, can change this instrumental attitude and make the learning experience much more pleasant and meaningful[7].

Although similar initiatives are very popular in other countries (i.e. France, USA, and Italy), in the UK, process drama and theatre are only occasionally present in higher education institution syllabi. I hope to have demonstrated that these methods can strongly enrich the learning experience thanks to the creative and imaginative use of the foreign language.

References

Carson, L. (2012). The role of drama in task-based learning: agency, identity and autonomy. *Scenario, 2012*(2), 47-60. http://publish.ucc.ie/journals/scenario/2012/2012-02/scenario-2012-02.pdf?

DICE. (2010). *Making a world of difference. A DICE resource for practitioners on educational theatre and drama*. DICE Consortium. http://www.dramanetwork.eu/

Dewey, J. (1938). *Experience and education*. Kappa Delta Pi.

Dougill, J. (1987). *Drama activities for language learning*. Macmillan.

Dunn, J. (2016). Demystifying process drama: exploring the why, what, and how. *Drama Australia Journal*, 40(2), 127-140.

---

[7]. As previously said, assessments in both activities were planned in form of oral exams, which were however received very positively, putting the students at ease.

Fonio, F. (2012). Stuffed pants! Staging full-scale comic plays with students of Italian as a foreign language. *Scenario, 2*, 17-26.

Giebert, S. (2014). Drama and theatre in teaching foreign languages for professional purposes. *Researching and Teaching Languages for Specific Purposes, 33*(1).

Guerra, M., & Militello, R. (2011). *Tra scuola e teatro. Per una didattica dei laboratori teatrali a scuola*. Angeli.

Hulse B., & Owens, A. (2017). Process drama as a tool for teaching modern languages. *Innovation in Language Learning and Teaching, 13*(1), 17-30. https://doi.org/10.1080/17501229.2017.1281928

Jun, L. (2001). Process drama in second- and foreign-language. In G. Bräuer (Ed.), *Body and language. Intercultural learning through drama* (pp. 51-70). Ablex Publishing.

Kao, S. M., & O'Neill, C. (1998). *Words into worlds: learning a second language through process drama*. Ablex Publishing Corporation.

Marini-Maio, N., & Ryan-Scheutz, C. (2010). *Set the stage! Teaching Italian through theatre. Theories, methods and practices*. Yale University Press.

O'Neill, C. (1995). *Drama worlds: a framework for process drama*. Heinemann.

Piazzoli, E. (2010). Process drama and intercultural language learning: an experience of contemporary Italy. *Research in Drama Education, 15*(3), 385-402. https://doi.org/10.1080/13569783.2010.495272

Pirola, C. (2011). Process drama e l'affascinante ruolo dell'insegnante: come insegnare una lingua facendo teatro. *Italiano LinguaDue, 1*, 463-483.

Ryan-Scheutz, C., & Colangelo, L. (2004). Full-scale theater production and foreign language learning. *Foreign Language Annals, 37*(3), 374-385. https://doi.org/10.1111/j.1944-9720.2004.tb02696.x

7 The European University Tandem project – an integrated online platform to foster intercultural language exchanges across Europe (and beyond)

Anke Bohm[1], Veronika Koeper-Saul[2], and Christian Mossmann[3]

Abstract

Language learning in tandem exchanges offers students a wealth of learning opportunities that are characterised by reciprocal and autonomous learning and foster authentic communication (Brammerts, 2001). Increasingly, these encounters take place online and, in this context, the EU-funded European University Tandem (EUniTa) project developed an integrated online platform which is specifically targeted at university students. Based on Web Real-Time Communications (WebRTC) technology, the platform offers students the chance to find a tandem partner and work with a range of materials designed to support the tandem exchanges. In this article, we will outline some key principles of learning in online tandem exchanges, introduce the main features of the EUniTa platform and discuss the development of the materials which were designed to foster students' Basic Interpersonal Communication Skills (BICS) and Cognitive Academic Language Proficiency (CALP).

Keywords: tandem exchanges, technology-enhanced learning, collaborative learning, autonomous learning.

1. University of Liverpool, Liverpool, England; abohm@liverpool.ac.uk

2. University of Liverpool, Liverpool, England; vkoeper@liverpool.ac.uk

3. University of Exeter, Exeter, England; c.mossmann@exeter.ac.uk

How to cite this chapter: Bohm, A., Koeper-Saul, V., & Mossmann, C. (2019). The European University Tandem project – an integrated online platform to foster intercultural language exchanges across Europe (and beyond). In N. Becerra, R. Biasini, H. Magedera-Hofhansl & A. Reimão (Eds), *Innovative language teaching and learning at university: a look at new trends* (pp. 53-61). Research-publishing.net. https://doi.org/10.14705/rpnet.2019.32.902

Chapter 7

1. Introduction

Tandem exchanges are a popular means to offer university students additional ways to practise their foreign language skills outside the classroom. Increasingly, tandem encounters take place online, and in this context, the EUniTa project developed an integrated platform for students to take part in language exchanges with students from partner universities. The project has been financially supported by the European Union under the Erasmus+ Programme between October 2015 and March 2018, and involved seven partner universities from five European countries – University of Exeter, University of Florence, Goethe University Frankfurt, University of Liverpool, Paris Sorbonne University, University of Poitiers and Blanquerna, and Universitat Ramon Llull. The platform can be viewed at www.eunita.org.

2. Characteristics of (online) tandem exchanges

The EUniTa platform for online tandem exchanges is characterised by a number of principles that generally apply to tandem learning settings. One of these principles is reciprocity (Brammerts, 2001), which highlights that tandem participants form a learning partnership and communicate as peers, alternating between the role of language learner and language expert. The principle of reciprocity presupposes that both partners possess competences which the other would like to learn (Augustin, 2011, p. 273), hence promoting the idea of cooperative learning (Funk, Gerlach, & Spaniel-Weise, 2017, p. 12). Brammerts (2001) further highlights learner autonomy as a defining principle of tandem learning. Autonomy represents a legitimate and desirable goal of language education (Benson, 2001, p. 2) and tandem exchanges give learners control over how to conduct the sessions as well as responsibility for their own learning. Learners decide which topics to discuss and which materials to use. They can negotiate their approach to feedback and error correction. Furthermore, tandem learning has the potential to foster intercultural learning even if it has been argued that this is less of a principle and more of a description of the relationship involved in the tandem exchange (Woodin, 2018, p. 10).

Online tandems share the same principles as face-to-face tandems and "focus learners on actively engaging in a foreign language community [whilst] exploiting the advantages of digital media" (Funk et al., 2017, p. 34). While the Internet has been used for the purpose of tandem exchanges since the mid-1990s – back then in the form of email (Cziko, 2004, p. 32) –, current technology allows for the use of synchronous videoconferencing technology, emulating face-to-face tandems more closely.

The fact that learning in tandem settings is characterised by a number of attributes that language educators generally like to promote in language teaching and learning contexts, such as learner autonomy, collaborative approaches to learning, or authentic language encounters, explains why tandem exchanges tend to be promoted widely by language departments and institution-wide language provisions. In light of technological advancements and due to the fact that it can be difficult to find a sufficient number of native speakers on campus, conducting tandem exchanges online has the potential to engage an increasing number of students in tandem learning. In this context, the EUniTa project developed an online platform to capitalise on this potential and foster online student tandem exchanges.

3. Features of the EUniTa platform

While there is a range of online platforms available for tandem exchanges, EUniTa is the only platform specifically created for university students that provides academic-related subject-specific material. This exclusive character of EUniTa supports university-level conversations and creates a safer environment for its users by restricting access to students from the participating partner universities[4].

EUniTa offers an integrated platform based on WebRTC technology which enables users to have their tandem without the need of employing additional

---

4. This is intended to prevent misuse (e.g. harassment) since user identities are easily traceable and any misuse of the platform can be acted upon immediately.

Chapter 7

media (see Figure 1). It is accessible on PCs and mobile devices alike due to its adaptive interface.

Figure 1. EUniTa features[5]

When registering and creating a profile, students are asked to provide their language level. In order to facilitate this, the platform contains a self-assessment test to determine language levels according to the Common European Framework of Reference (CEFR, Council of Europe, 2001). Having data on the students' language levels is also important for the automatic tandem matching process, which allows an efficient way of bringing users together.

An up-to-date timeline (see Figure 2) allows students to keep a record of their tandem activities and can support them if they decide to make use of the platform's option to receive a certificate.

For the matching process, a set of hard and soft criteria is employed. The term 'hard criteria' refers to the set of criteria that needs to be fully met in order for

---

5. Materials from the EUniTa platform are reproduced with kind permissions from © EUniTa, EU Non-Proliferation Consortium eLearning, as per their terms of use; https://www.eunita.org/

the system to match two users in a tandem, whereas 'soft criteria' describes a collection of criteria that optimise the created tandem further. The former includes the target language and the language offered. Should a student want to improve their language skills, especially within their academic field or subject area, they can tick a box to that effect when registering for a tandem and would then only be paired with somebody who has the same objective. Soft criteria, on the other hand, include the same language level for both target and offered language as well as the same expectations with regards to the frequency of learning, topics to be discussed, and age of both tandem partners.

Figure 2.   Timeline

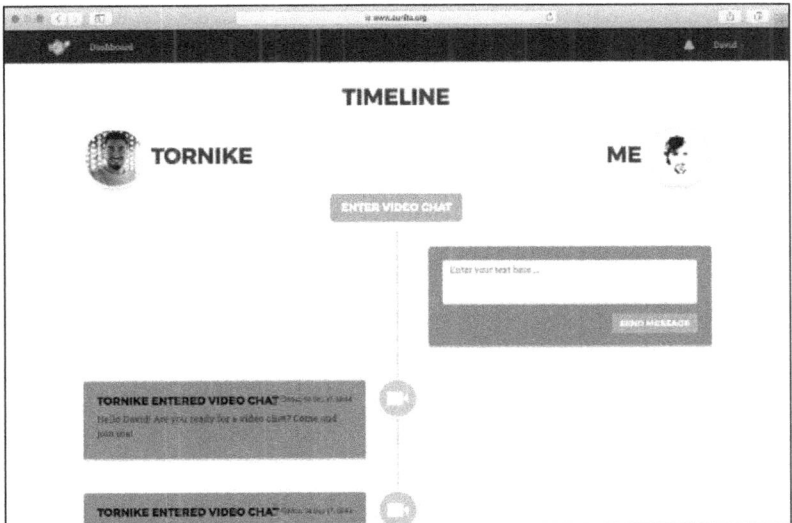

4.   BICS and CALP materials

As the EUniTa platform matches participants for general as well as academic language exchanges, two types of materials are offered: BICS guides to improve *basic interpersonal communication skills* and CALP guides to help build *cognitive academic language proficiency*. BICS is the context-embedded

Chapter 7

language necessary for day-to-day interaction and informal conversations, whilst CALP is necessary to understand and discuss more abstract language with few, if any, non-verbal cues (see de Wit, 2015, referring to Cummins, 1979). BICS covers all levels of the CEFR, whilst CALP – for which at least five years of learning are required to reach full proficiency (Cummins, 2016, p. 942) – correlates with the higher levels only, starting from B2. Consequently, the platform offers CALP material only at B and C levels, whilst BICS covers the whole range (see Figure 3).

Figure 3. Library drop-down menu of EUniTa materials

Titel	Level	Prep.	Language				
Cinema	A2	No	Deutsch	English	Español	Français	Italiano
Cinema B1	B1	No	Deutsch	English	Español	Français	Italiano
Cinema B2	B2	No	Deutsch	English	Español	Français	Italiano
Cinema C1	C1	No	Deutsch	English	Español	Français	Italiano

- Society
- Daily Life
- Me & the Others
- Studies and Careers
- Culture
  - Architecture
  - Books & Authors
  - Films & TV
- Food & Recipes
- Museums
- Music
- Stereotypes
- Health & Sports
- Places & Spaces
- Academic Topics (CALP)

To respond to the greater demand for BICS, there are 151 worksheets on 41 topics across seven categories[6] and six CEFR levels, each available in six languages. Each topic includes worksheets on different levels to allow students to monitor

---

6. For category titles see the top level titles in the screenshot above.

their progress. A typical worksheet such as 'Living in another country' at A2 level (CEFR), on the topic 'Moving Countries' within the category 'Studies and Careers', will have a general topic particularly relevant for university students and will set off with a preparatory task designed to recall or look up relevant vocabulary. On lower levels, some basic phrases are provided, but there is no link to a dictionary, since the students are meant to work out relevant vocabulary with the help of each other.

The main tasks would include application of grammar and phrases typical for the level, such as likes and dislikes or the opportunity to use past tenses at A2. There is no integrated grammar on EUniTa: users are meant to apply in conversation what they have learnt before; the goal is to improve speaking and interaction skills.

For CALP conversations, EUniTa offers worksheets on 34 topics within three broad disciplines: Humanities, Natural and Medical Sciences, and Social Sciences. Here again, the principle of collaborative learning truly comes into play: the partners are relied on for technical terms and subject-/discipline-specific expertise, and this is made possible by matching students from similar disciplines. What the sheets offer are suggestions as to how to start collecting and exchanging these terms as well as support for practising communicative functions required in academic and professional contexts, e.g. presentations, discussions and debates, data interpretation, or providing critical feedback.

For example, the worksheet on 'Intercultural Communication' within the 'Humanities' category (https://www.eunita.org/files/materials/181_en_GB.pdf) links to authentic materials in which abstract topics, e.g. Saxonic, Teutonic, Gallic, and Nipponic intellectual styles are discussed. Authentic means that each sheet will link to material in the respective target language and thus worksheets on the same topic, but in different languages, may link to different original material such as graphs, videos, or articles. Analysing, discussing, contrasting, and comparing such materials will not only help to unearth the relevant subject vocabulary, but also to improve communicative functions. To encourage further independent learning, the worksheets may conclude with a follow-up activity, such as inviting users to find another article on the given topic in their own language and discussing it with the partner at their next tandem meeting.

5. Conclusion

According to Cziko (2004, p. 38), the growth of technology has increased the need of foreign languages and cultures while at the same time providing new means and resources by which this knowledge can be obtained. In this context, language learning in online tandems represents an innovative way of exploiting technology to offer students the opportunity to engage in non-formal language learning in authentic, reciprocal, and intercultural communication settings. The EuniTa platform constitutes a new online tandem provider in this regard, matching university students with each other to enable them to engage in language exchanges. In addition to offering participants automatic matching and an integrated platform, EUniTa also provides a wealth of tandem learning materials, which have been designed not only to foster interpersonal communication skills, but, crucially, also cognitive academic language proficiency.

In the next phase of the project, we will evaluate to what extent and in what manner participants are making use of the EUniTa platform, its features and the materials on offer. It will be interesting to observe if students manage to engage in successful exchanges, being able to negotiate the exchange entirely autonomously and reciprocally. In terms of development, the project is also looking to expand the number of partner universities and diversify the host countries involved in order to grow the platform, open it to an increasing number of students, and add further languages.

Acknowledgements

We would like to thank the European Union for providing funding for the EUniTa Project as well as our project partners and the students involved in the platform development.

References

Augustin, W. (2011). *Kooperativer Fremdsprachenerwerb im Teletandem. Grundlagen der Lehr- und Lernmethode.* https://publications.ub.uni-mainz.de/theses/volltexte/2012/3131/pdf/3131.pdf

Benson, P. (2001). *Teaching and researching autonomy in language learning.* Pearson Education.

Brammerts, H. (2001). Autonomes Sprachenlernen im Tandem: Entwicklung eines Konzepts. In H. Brammerts & K. Kleppin (Eds), *Selbstgesteuertes Sprachenlernen im Tandem: ein Handbuch* (pp. 9-16). Stauffenburg.

Council of Europe. (2001). *Common European framework of references for languages: learning, teaching, assessment.* Cambridge University Press.

Cummins, J. (1979). Cognitive/academic language proficiency, linguistic interdependence, the optimum age question and some other matters. *Working Papers on Bilingualism, 19,* 121-129.

Cummins, J. (2016). Reflections on Cummins (1980), The cross-lingual dimensions of language proficiency: implications for bilingual education and the optimal age issue. *TESOL Quarterly, 50*(4), 940-944. https://doi.org/10.1002/tesq.339

Cziko, G. (2004). Electronic tandem language learning (eTandem): a third approach to second language learning for the 21st century. *CALICO Journal, 22*(1), 25-39. https://doi.org/10.1558/cj.v22i1.25-39

De Wit, A.-L. (2015). Teaching tips: understanding BICS and CALP. *University of the Witwatersrand, Johannesburg, Articles on Language* [online]. http://www.witslanguageschool.com/NewsRoom/ArticleView/tabid/180/ArticleId/285/Teaching-tips-Understanding-BICS-and-CALP.aspx

Funk, H., Gerlach, M., & Spaniel-Weise, D. (2017). *Handbook for foreign language learning in online tandems and educational settings.* Peter Lang. https://doi.org/10.3726/b10732

Woodin, J. (2018). *Interculturality, interaction and language learning. Insights from tandem partnerships.* Routledge. https://doi.org/10.4324/9781315640525

8 Becoming a more active and creative language learner with digital tools

Mikiko Kurose[1]

Abstract

Interacting with peers can be difficult for some students, due to their personality as well as to their learning styles. This paper shows how the Task-Based Approach (TBA) can be implemented and how digital resources can be used in language teaching and learning to enhance the students' experience and foster autonomy. To do so, I describe tasks I implemented for university students at A2/B1 level Japanese – Common European Framework of Reference (CEFR) – delivered to a group of mainly Chinese students. Chinese students seem to be reluctant to speak up and share their opinions in class (Wu, 2015), which needed to be addressed in language classes. In order to encourage them to be more active and creative, TBA was deployed to help students perform tasks while using authentic materials, including online materials as well as digital tools to give more exposure to natural language. By adopting this method, language learning can be more heuristic for learners to achieve their learning goals, and students can be more engaged and motivated in tasks. At the same time, it was observed that students became more proactive to use pre-learned language in more contextualised situations and showed more originality as a result.

Keywords: task-based, digital resources, motivation, creativity, autonomy.

---

1. University of Nottingham, Nottingham, England; mikiko.kurose@nottingham.ac.uk

How to cite this chapter: Kurose, M. (2019). Becoming a more active and creative language learner with digital tools. In N. Becerra, R. Biasini, H. Magedera-Hofhansl & A. Reimão (Eds), *Innovative language teaching and learning at university: a look at new trends* (pp. 63-71). Research-publishing.net. https://doi.org/10.14705/rpnet.2019.32.903

Chapter 8

1. Introduction

1.1. Rationale

The Japanese language attracts many Chinese speakers compared to other nationals as it has adopted Chinese characters, which gives a certain advantage to Chinese speakers (Tamaoka, 2014, p. 432). From my classroom observations, however, Chinese students seem to be rather passive learners who find it difficult to share opinions and hesitate to ask questions and participate in discussions. This may be due to "the extremely exam-oriented" culture (Taguchi, Magid, & Papi, 2009, p. 69), whereby the purpose of learning is to pass exams by memorising and practising what is presented in class to anticipate what may come up in the exam. This seems to be one of the contributing factors for certain East-Asian students losing motivation when learning languages (Taguchi et al., 2009). Wu's (2015) study also shows how Chinese learners, especially those from the mainland, are expected to sit in class quietly rather than actively participate. In this paper, I demonstrate how, by using a TBA to devise tasks that encourage students to interact with each other and create an environment in which students feel comfortable, this passive learning behaviour can be gently overcome and students can be encouraged to vocalise their opinions and ask questions.

1.2. Task-based approach

Johnson (1995) highlights how the significance of the learners' academic, cultural, and personal background affects conversational competencies in class and argues that teaching should encompass the learners' *real operating conditions*, i.e. real-life situations. This seems particularly relevant in this case, where due to cultural factors of the type discussed by Johnson (1995), the Chinese students are reluctant to participate in simple oral communication in class, even creating own sentences from prompts, describing photos, let alone in discussions and debates. Therefore, a combination of the teaching methods of Presenting, Practising, and Producing (PPP) (Long, 2015) and Task-Based Language Teaching (TBLT) was adopted to foster a learning environment that would encourage working with peers to enhance oral communication and to self-correct.

TBLT is defined by Ellis (2003) as "teaching that is based entirely on tasks" (p. 351) and tasks are identified by six essential features:

- a task is a workplan,
- a task involves a primary focus on meaning,
- a task involves real-world processes of language use,
- a task can involve any of the four language skills,
- a task engages cognitive processes,
- a task has a clearly defined communicative outcome (Ellis, 2003, pp. 9-10).

According to Ellis (2003), "a task is a workplan" (p. 9) that has an intended outcome which is interrelated with PPP methods. PPP is more explicitly focussed on grammatical forms, whereas TBLT focusses on meaning (Willis, 1996). By combining both approaches, students are encouraged to produce output while experimenting with language to work towards a goal. Learners, therefore, are given tasks which motivate and promote more active participation. Tasks given in class are contextualised, for example, within situations that learners may encounter outside the classroom. However, rather than acquiring the particular language elements that the teacher intends, there is a danger that the focus of learning may go astray during completion of the task. To bridge this gap, the approach presented here has been developed. It is referred to as TBA to differentiate it from TBLT, which, as discussed, combines features of TBLT and PPP. More precisely, PPP is grammar and structure practice which Asian students are familiar with and it transfers that knowledge in a more contextualised way. TBA, in this case, provides more opportunities to practise oral communication skills and to use language in more ad-hoc or authentic situations.

2. Tasks

Four task-based projects incorporating digital tools were designed for Asian exchange students who study Japanese in the UK. These are described in the

Chapter 8

following sections. The students were predominantly speakers of Chinese who had four contact hours weekly. Their language level was between CEFR A2 and B1.

2.1. Task 1: about yourself

Figure 1. Fakebook

A website called Fakebook (www.classtools.net/FB/home-page, Figure 1) was used to write a blog online as a more realistic way to introduce themselves. Students were then asked to view the pages of at least three peers with whom they did not usually associate, and give comments on their posts. Students needed to use the plain form of Japanese (casual tone of language) to reinforce their learning. Students were given further tasks to write and interact with fellow students, such as sharing their feelings regarding studying abroad and their plans for Christmas, where they could ask questions to peers in a more spontaneous manner.

Regular feedback, comments, and corrections were posted by the teacher. The online presentation board software Padlet (padlet.com) was used to access each other's Fakebook pages as it requires a password to write comments.

2.2. Task 2: cultural comparison

Figure 2. Padlet

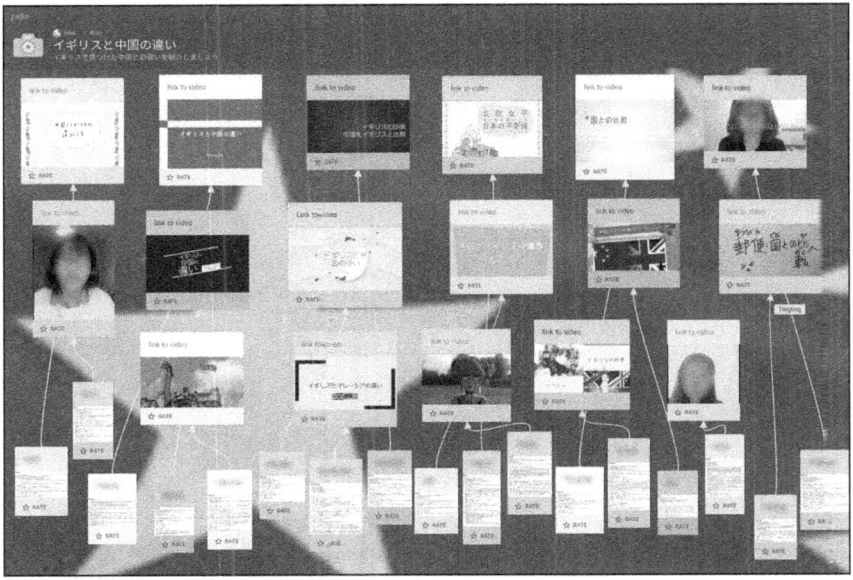

In this task, students were asked to produce a video on cultural similarities and differences, in this case between China/Malaysia and the UK. Students made a video on their mobile phones, used video editing tools, PowerPoint presentations,

Chapter 8

and subtitle editing tools, which showed real engagement with the task. Pre-learned language elements were fully used to complete the task and even as yet unlearned grammatical elements were used as students were eager to improve their videos. Videos and teacher feedback were collated using Padlet (Figure 2), and all students' videos were stored in the university OneDrive and then linked to the Padlet board to share.

In class, all students viewed the videos, which also served as a good listening exercise, and shared their opinions and feelings, as well as giving suggestions for improvement.

2.3. Task 3: travel

The students organised a fictional trip within a set budget for a small group holiday, giving reasons for the trip, the itinerary, useful tips, and a breakdown of the budget. The final presentation was a PowerPoint video to narrate their travel plans. Students were told to use authentic online information (e.g. https://travel.yahoo.co.jp/) to plan, and all discussions with peers were in Japanese throughout. Therefore, ad-hoc use of language was encouraged, and planning the trip also fostered problem solving.

The students' presentations were viewed by peers in class, and some students actually went on the trip they planned. This proves that the task was beneficial for the students, and their language skills were used for a real purpose.

2.4. Task 4: university life

In this task, students were asked to describe daily problems in university life in the UK. They were asked to use a digital resource online (www.storyboardthat.com, Figure 3) to display a problem, and peers were asked to give advice and/or solutions in Japanese. The digital resource was a form of story board which is similar to manga (Japanese comic books) thus incorporating a cultural element to the task. The storyboard had six scenes which described problems, and students had to think about how to form, summarise, or elaborate on a story.

Figure 3. Storyboard[2]

Informal discussions took place after the initial presentation of the problem, which encouraged students to give advice and find solutions using colloquial language. Students welcomed this chance to experiment using informal and colloquial language which may be heard in Japanese anime (cartoons) or dramas in order to express their spur-of-the-moment feelings and opinions. This positive feedback was captured through an end of semester questionnaire.

3. Outcomes and reflection

The initial aim of TBA was to get students, especially Chinese, involved and interacting more in class to make the most of their language learning experience. By using TBA, it was hoped that they would become more active language learners. As a result of combining TBA and various types of technology, students were more motivated, engaged, and became more proactive about their learning.

---

2. © 2019 - Clever Prototypes, LLC. Reproduced with kind permissions from the copyright holder as per their website's guidelines: https://www.storyboardthat.com/help-and-faqs/storyboard-copyright-faq

Chapter 8

They used textbooks and online materials to complete tasks and critically sourced and selected information needed. Through the completion of the tasks, the students commented in the survey as well as in their module evaluation, that the tasks made them use more grammar and vocabulary, they gained more confidence in speaking, the variety of tasks were enjoyable, and they learned skills beyond language learning such as editing videos.

Methods of presentation were kept to a minimum, e.g. videos and PowerPoint presentations. However, the students went beyond expectations by taking their audience into account. To help listeners understand unknown vocabulary and phrases in the presentation, they added subtitles and also ensured coherence of content. The students also added, in their feedback, that they felt that they had practised more oral skills in the pre-recorded way of presentation, as they could rectify their own mistakes and practise their pronunciation until they were satisfied.

4. Conclusions

We recognise the importance of embedding practical experience in language learning task design in order to enable students to transfer their knowledge to suit their needs (Long, 2015, p. 68). As shown in the above study, carefully designed tasks can motivate students. As students became more involved in tasks, they took full ownership of their learning and worked actively in small groups in achieving goals. Anecdotally, some students even went on the trips they planned in class. In my experience with this cohort, the TBA enabled students' confidence to experiment with language, to show their originality, and to share opinions in group communication. Learners' problem solving and reflection skills were also required during the process of completing tasks by thought-out editing of final videos and presentations. This heuristic approach to teaching and learning was beneficial overall for Chinese learners as it helped them to become more active language learners and able to use language for their needs in the real world, to share their opinions, and to overcome the exam-oriented passive learning style to which they had become accustomed to in their home countries.

Acknowledgements

I would like to thank my students from the Ningbo campus of University of Nottingham.

References

Ellis, R. (2003). *Task-based language learning and teaching*. Oxford.
Johnson, K. E. (1995). *Understanding communication in second language classrooms*. Cambridge University Press.
Long, M. (2015). *Second language acquisition and task-based language teaching*. Wiley Blackwell.
Taguchi, T., Magid M., & Pap:, M. (2009). The L2 motivational self system among Japanese, Chinese and Iranian learner of English: a comparative study. In Z. Dörnyei & E. Ushioda (Eds), *Motivation, language identity and the L2 self*. Bristol. https://doi.org/10.21832/9781847691293-005
Tamaoka, K. (2014). The Japanese writing system and lexical understanding. *Japanese Language and Literature, 48*(2), 431-471. http://www.jstor.org/stable/24394417
Willis, J. (1996). A flexible framework for task-based learning. In J. Willis & D. Willis (Eds), *Challenge and change in language teaching* (pp. 52-62). Macmillan Education.
Wu, Q. (2015). Re-examining the "Chinese learner": a case study of mainland chinese students' learning experiences at british universities. *Higher Education, 70*(4), 753-766. https://doi.org/10.1007/s10734-015-9865-y

9. Incorporating D2L and Google Docs in language teaching and learning

Miao Li[1]

Abstract

The present paper discusses ways of incorporating two digital tools, Desire2Learn (D2L) and Google Docs, in language teaching and learning. Data were collected from four French language modules offered at the University of Calgary. Through the analysis of the tutor's observations and module evaluations, this paper explores the effectiveness of these tools in helping learners and instructors to move beyond the walls of the classrooms, and to work towards creating an active and learner-oriented environment. Results obtained reveal that both tools contributed to creating an inclusive learning environment and facilitated student participation and instructor's feedback. The author suggests that some pedagogical interventions could be applied to enhance the effectiveness of these tools.

Keywords: D2L, Google Docs, nclusive, active, learner-oriented.

1. Introduction

Teaching French language modules in a multicultural university in Canada presents challenges due to the relatively large size of the beginner-level classes and the various cultural and learning backgrounds of students. In order to increase student participation and to create a tailored and active learning experience, this

---

1. University of Calgary, Calgary, Canada; miao.li@ucalgary.ca

How to cite this chapter: Li, M. (2019). Incorporating D2L and Google Docs in language teaching and learning. In N. Becerra, R. Biasini, H. Magedera-Hofhansl & A. Reimão (Eds), *Innovative language teaching and learning at university: a look at new trends* (pp. 73-81). Research-publishing.net. https://doi.org/10.14705/rpnet.2019.32.904

Chapter 9

paper proposes the incorporation of the Virtual Learning Environment (VLE) platform D2L and Google Docs in French language classes offered at the University of Calgary, in line with current pedagogical approaches (Hockings, 2010; McGuire, 2015) that promote innovative language teaching and learning practices. The modules align with the Common European Framework of Reference (CEFR) levels as follows: A1-A2, A2, B2, and C1.

2. D2L, Google Docs, and language learning

2.1. Creating an inclusive, synchronized, and collaborative learning environment

When we walk into a classroom, we often notice a tapestry of cultural and social backgrounds that anticipates the same level of inclusiveness. Critical pedagogues like Hockings (2010, p. 2) maintain that as a tutor, being inclusive means actively acknowledging students, being mindful of their academic needs, and adequately guiding and supporting them on their academic journeys, regardless of their backgrounds, prior knowledge, and more. Hockings (2010) highlights practices that support an inclusive teaching environment. For instance, learning about individual students, creating a safe, respectful, and open-minded learning environment, addressing individual needs, and challenging existing policies, practices, and systems that exclude certain students (Hockings, 2010, pp. 46-47). Digital tools such as VLEs like D2L and Google Docs may facilitate the application of these pedagogical strategies.

D2L (https://www.d2l.com/) is a virtual learning management system widely used in Canadian universities. Like all VLEs, this online platform creates a virtual space where the instructor can manage students' grades, post news, and learning materials, design online quizzes and assignments, and engage with students in the discussion forums. Depending on tutors' teaching styles and their familiarity with technology, these functions are used unevenly in classes, and especially in the modules here analysed. To tackle this issue, I embarked on a more active use of D2L. For instance, in module C1, to encourage more participation and use of

D2L, I started by building a rapport with students prior to the first class of the module. As an icebreaker, I sent a welcome message in the discussion forum and invited students to introduce their study programme(s), hobbies, and expectations of the module. It helped me to get to know students on an individual basis, and to slightly adjust teaching style and module content in order to meet their needs and expectations. According to Glazer (2016), this established rapport between tutor and students also allows to foster a learning environment beneficial for students' collaboration in and outside the class. During the semester, I used D2L to engage in a consistent dialogue with students, for instance about assignments and module content, in order to explore and add new dimensions to the module-related topics (see supplementary material, part 1).

Figure 1. Using Google Docs for an in-class grammar activity (A2)

> **P.133 Ex. 11**
>
> **Groupe 1:** Jacques Cartier (1491-1557) est l'un des grands explorateurs français. Il naquit (est né) à Saint-Malo en 1491. Dans sa jeunesse, il alla (est allé) au Portugal, au Brésil et probablement dans la région de Terre-Neuve. En 1534, le roi de France lui donna (a donné) la mission d'explorer les côtes de l'Amérique du Nord. Cartier et ses hommes partirent (sont partis) de Saint-Malo le 20 avril et arrivèrent (sont arrivés) dans la région de Gaspé au Canada le 25 juillet.
>
> **Groupe 2:** Cartier descendit (est descendu) à terre, planta (a planté) une croix dans le sol et prit (a pris) possession de la région au nom du roi de France. L'expédition revint (est revenue) en France où elle fut (a été) reçue en triomphe. Jacques Cartier fit (a fait) un second voyage en 1535 avec la mission cette fois de chercher de l'or et des pierres précieuses.
>
> **Groupe 3:** Il n' trouva (a pas trouvé) d'or mais il découvrit (a découvert) un immense fleuve qu'il nomma (a nommé) Saint-Laurent. Cartier remonta (est remonté) le fleuve jusqu'au site d'un village indien, Hochelaga, aujourd'hui Montréal. Les premiers colons français s'installèrent (se sont installés) au Canada 70 ans plus tards. C'est ainsi que le Canada devint (est devenu) un territoire français.
>
> Pour plus d'informations sur le passé simple, lisez:
> https://www.podcastfrancaisfacile.com/cours/passe-simple-lecon-francais-facile.html
> http://www.alloprof.qc.ca/BV/pages/f1191.aspx

Chapter 9

To provide a synchronized and collaborative learning environment, in A1-A2 and A2, I created a shared Google Docs for each class to use throughout the semester. Through this tool, I had instant access to students' input during the in-class group activities (see Figure 1 above). Therefore, I was able to target and approach the group(s) or individuals in need of guidance in a timely manner. These informal and frequent assessments allowed me to provide feedback and adjust teaching practices when necessary.

2.2. Fostering an active learning environment through task-based activities and learner-oriented discussions

As Ambrose et al. (2010) and McGuire (2015) argue, active learning encourages student engagement in contrast to a more passive environment that can be found in a lecture-based classroom. Research has clearly shown that active learning techniques, such as concept maps, debates, discussions, games, peer instruction and/or reviews, pooling, and role playing can be more effective than other teaching techniques as they contribute to the generation of comprehension and retention of concepts (Handelsman, Miller, & Pfund, 2007). Using digital tools, the tutor may find it easier to employ the above learning techniques in larger size classes, or to propose active learning outside the classroom.

In A2, Google Docs was used to propose a more creative activity (Figure 2). I generated a shopping list with a Google Doc, divided students in groups of four and asked them to shop on the French version of the Canadian Walmart website (https://www.walmart.ca/fr). At the end of this activity, I selected two winners amongst the groups, under the following criteria: one for being the fastest to add all the products in the shopping cart, and the other for finding the products with the lowest total estimate. Defining the winners using two different criteria kept students motivated and engaged even when some groups had already completed their task. This activity helped learners to reflect on how module content may fit into their daily life, and offered a new way to act in their enhancement of new vocabulary and expressions.

Figure 2. Using Google Docs for a task-based learning activity (A2)

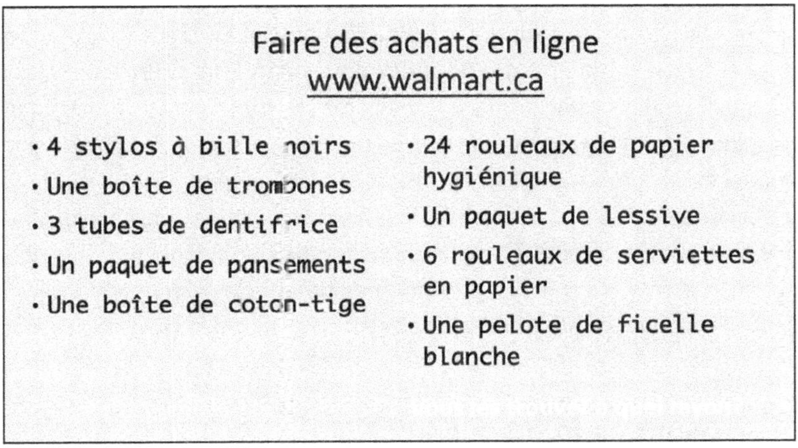

Faire des achats en ligne
www.walmart.ca

- 4 stylos à bille noirs
- Une boîte de trombones
- 3 tubes de dentifrice
- Un paquet de pansements
- Une boîte de coton-tige
- 24 rouleaux de papier hygiénique
- Un paquet de lessive
- 6 rouleaux de serviettes en papier
- Une pelote de ficelle blanche

In B2, Google Docs allowed to keep track of all activities completed outside of class. For instance, in this course where after-class readings are frequently involved, I assigned paragraphs to each student, with a content table to be completed (vocabulary, summary, grammar) in Google Docs (see supplementary material, part 2). Each student was also asked to propose a discussion topic derived from their reading. For those who were less fluent in French, having access to the discussion topics allowed them to prepare ahead and to feel more confident when engaging in discussions in class. Furthermore, I could easily correct and comment on students' answers in the document, and highlight important content for them to review. D2L discussion forums were used in C1 for graded reading assignments (see supplementary material, part 3). Students asked and answered questions of each other to generate new ideas and enhance their comprehension of the text. Through this task, they took an active role in their learning, developed their critical thinking, and learned from each other.

In language classrooms, students are likely to have different preferred activities, a challenge addressed by the universal design for learning (Rose et al., 2006). The universal design for learning provides significant guidance supporting "multiple means of representation, […] expression, and […] engagement" (Rose et al.,

2006, pp. 3-4). Such an approach finds an ideal application in the digital context. For example, when teaching pronouns, I proposed two types of practice (see supplementary material, part 4): (1) a rather traditional exercise, where students rewrite a sentence by replacing underlined elements with a pronoun, and (2) another that prompts students to use grammar in real-life contexts. Either activity allows them to review a grammatical point. However, proposing two options increases the flexibility and variety in students' learning experiences, allowing them to choose the activity that suits their level and interest, thus taking a more active role in their learning. Completing such activities in Google Docs enables students to access classmates' answers, providing them with opportunities for peer correction and positive competition.

3. Results and discussion

The outcomes of these digitally enhanced learning strategies are based on the observations of the students in class, as well as on module evaluations at the end of the semester (Table 1).

Table 1. Students' evaluation on the overall instruction in three modules, compared with the average rating of the Faculty of Arts (evaluation of C1 fall 2018 is not available yet)

	Faculty (Winter 2018)	A1-A2 (Winter 2018)	B2 (Winter 2018)	Faculty (Spring 2018)	A2 (Spring 2018)
Rating (out of 7)	5.97	6.53	6.11	6.11	6.50
Enrolment	N/A	34	10	N/A	16
Valid instruments received	N/A	31	9	N/A	12
Response rate	N/A	90.18%	90%	N/A	75%

As there are no specific questions regarding students' experience of using D2L and Google Docs in the module evaluations, the above ratings do not necessarily reflect students' feedback regarding these tools. However, from their verbal and written comments cited below, some included in the open comments on the official module evaluations, it has become apparent that students appreciated (1) the learning environment ("comfortable learning environment", "class is engaged and interactive", "D2L is organized and D2L notes are very helpful"), and (2) the learning activities ("[the tutor] spends time and provides a lot of ways to know students' competences and weaknesses, offers many helpful resources", "[the tutor proposes] various activities, games, group work and speaking practices that facilitate learning and encourage participation", "[the tutor] uses technology", "group work on Google Docs is great for answering questions anonymously").

Out of a total of fifty-two students who submitted the module evaluations, four students provided negative feedback on Google Docs. In A1-A2, two students considered it to be ineffective and slow, another student found the simultaneous use of Google Docs in class to be anxiety inducing. In B2, one student pointed out the inconvenience of browsing information on Google Docs when the content is growing. This has led me to consider the differences of students' familiarity with technology, which may affect the use of digital tools in larger classes.

In C1, eighteen out of the twenty-four students participated in the D2L self-presentation, and almost everyone participated in the forum discussions. The slight increase showed that setting forum discussions as graded assignments (each 2%) slightly affects participation. Providing individual feedback to students' posts could have also encouraged their contribution, although it is time-consuming and could be unfeasible for larger classes. Finally, it is evident that the length and quality of students' input varied and were associated with their language proficiency, familiarity with the topic, and time to participate.

4. Conclusion

This paper underlined the role of D2L in providing an interactive learning space outside class, and the usefulness of Google Docs in fostering a synchronous and collaborative learning environment. Both tools facilitated efficient feedback and adjustments in teaching. The practice outcomes correspond largely with the literature presented in this paper in creating an active and learner-centred environment. Based on students' feedback and my self-reflection, the following changes will be implemented in my future pedagogical practice:

- for lengthy Google Docs, using a table of contents to facilitate students' viewing and retrieving of information;

- using only those functions that are in line with learning outcomes;

- explaining verbally and/or in writing the reasons and benefits of using these tools; and

- giving students time to familiarise themselves with these tools.

These changes should contribute towards students' better understanding of how digital tools are linked to the learning objectives. In the future, it would be helpful to investigate whether such changes will increase the effectiveness of these digital tools and how much further they improve students' academic performances.

Supplementary material

https://research-publishing.box.com/s/ntum021u8unzudctmgw7wbvycwfh1jia

References

Ambrose, S. A., Bridges, M. W., DiPietro, M., Lovett, M. C., & Norman, M. K. (2010). *How learning works: seven research-based principles for smart teaching*. Jossey-Bass

Glazer, R. A. (2016). Building rapport to improve retention and success in online classes. *Journal of Political Science Education, 12*(4), 437-456. https://doi.org/10.1080/15512169.2016.1155994

Handelsman, J., Miller, S., & Pfund, C. (2007). *Scientific teaching*. W. H. Freeman and Company.

Hockings, C. (2010). *Inclusive learning and teaching in higher education: a synthesis of research*. https://www.heacademy.ac.uk/system/files/inclusive_teaching_and_learning_in_he_synthesis_200410_0.pdf

McGuire, S. Y. (2015). *Teach students how to learn: strategies you can incorporate into any course to improve student metacognition, study skills, and motivation*. Stylus Publishing, LLC.

Rose, D., Harbour, W., Johnston, C. S., Daley, S., & Abarbanell, L. (2006). Universal design for learning in postsecondary education: reflections on principles and their application. *Journal of Postsecondary Education and Disability, 19*(2), 1-27.

# 10. Challenging, supporting, and empowering students in IWLP beginners' classes: a teaching and learning response to internationalisation

Alison Nader[1]

Abstract

Institution-Wide Language Programme (IWLP) modules are a popular option for international students at the University of Reading. Student feedback and module results show that some of these students face particular challenges in relation to their peers. In this paper, we describe how a team teaching Beginners French – Common European Framework of Reference (CEFR) level A1 – addressed this issue. More specifically, we focus on the development of a new module with integrated support and differentiated assessment as well as student feedback and suggestions for curriculum enhancement. We demonstrate how minor module and assessment modifications enabled the team to support students who might have dropped out or become discouraged and at the same time raise the level of challenge for all students whatever their background.

Keywords: internationalisation, diversity, assessment, student-led curriculum design.

1. Introduction

The increasing internationalisation of UK higher education poses opportunities and challenges for IWLPs. In 2016-2017, almost 33% of non-EU students in the

---

1. University of Reading, Reading, England; a.n.nader@reading.ac.uk

How to cite this chapter: Nader, A. (2019). Challenging, supporting, and empowering students in IWLP beginners' classes: a teaching and learning response to internationalisation. In N. Becerra, R. Biasini, H. Magedera-Hofhansl & A. Reimão (Eds), *Innovative language teaching and learning at university: a look at new trends* (pp. 83-93). Research-publishing.net. https://doi.org/10.14705/rpnet.2019.32.905

UK came from China (UKCISA, 2018). Teaching multicultural, multilingual groups of language learners together contributes to developing global graduates in addition to teaching language skills. As Dlaska (2013) argues, "[a] pedagogy which facilitates international encounters and collaboration […] puts the IWLP in a unique position to trial and advance the internationalisation of learning and teaching in the university" (p. 261).

This project addresses the challenge of increasing diversity by recognising that some students have a cultural and linguistic advantage, especially at the beginning of the course. We wanted to keep our diverse cohort together but at the same time address the particular challenges faced by East Asian students. The students we worked with were studying a 20 credit Beginners French module at the International Study and Language Institute of the University of Reading. The course sets 60 contact hours and another 140 hours of self-study which is supported by reading and listening material, made available on the virtual learning environment, and speaking and writing e-submission tasks.

Based on the results of previous cohorts and given the interactive nature of the lessons in an IWLP classroom, we decided to focus on supporting speaking and listening skills. Furthermore, we took into account that student anxiety is high for all students in these two skills (Gu, 2010), especially for those whose first language and prior learning experiences make French challenging. For these reasons, we made small changes to the syllabus and introduced scaffolded assessment. Furthermore, after securing university funding, we organised student-led focus groups to test some of our underlying assumptions and receive student input on the syllabus.

2. Method: the phases of the project

2.1. Phase 1 (2016 to 2017)

We obtained project funding to develop focussed listening, speaking, and pronunciation material and ran extra workshops for selected students. Having reviewed student feedback, the conclusion to this phase was that all students taking Beginners French could benefit from explicit skills teaching and that the materials and the timing of the sessions did not meet the needs of the weaker students.

The learning experience, early on, was leading to de-motivation and absenteeism among both Asian and European students. For the linguistic reasons highlighted above, the former often felt overwhelmed while the latter found the pace too slow. Even though all of our students were beginners, their prior experience, if not their formal learning, meant that they were not starting from the same baseline and therefore we needed to make some modifications in order to make the teaching equitable for all (Killick, 2017, p. 136).

One possibility was to create a separate module with different learning outcomes to cater for diversity, but this approach would have undermined our secondary aim of fostering multicultural awareness among our students.

2.2. Phase 2 (February to September 2017)

In this phase, we reviewed the syllabus and contact hours for the Beginners French module, LA1PF1, and designed a second module, Beginners French with Listening and Speaking Workshops, LA1PF9, referred to as F1 and F9 hereafter. We have run the two modules together since October 2017.

We continue to teach these rich, culturally mixed groups together, while recognising that some students need extra support, especially at the beginning of the course. For this reason, we have introduced a differentiated summative assessment task, which we describe below, and allocate students to either module following a placement test and not solely on the basis of their first language.

2.3. Implementing Phase 2 changes (October 2017 to May 2018)

All students taking IWLP F1 registered for the Beginners' module (Figure 1).

Figure 1. Students studying IWLP F1, 2017-2018, by nationality (66 students)

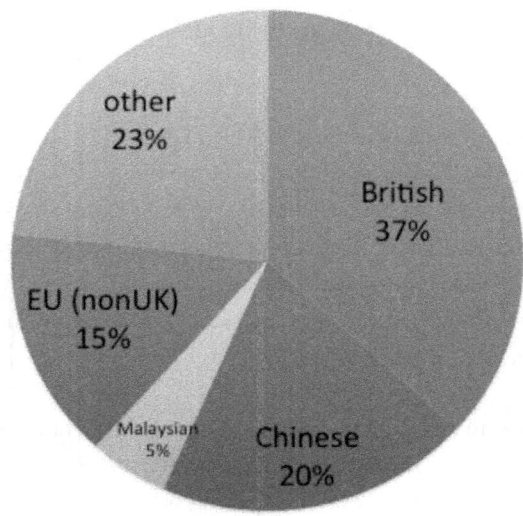

Figure 2. Standard IWLP F1, 2017-2018 (40 students)

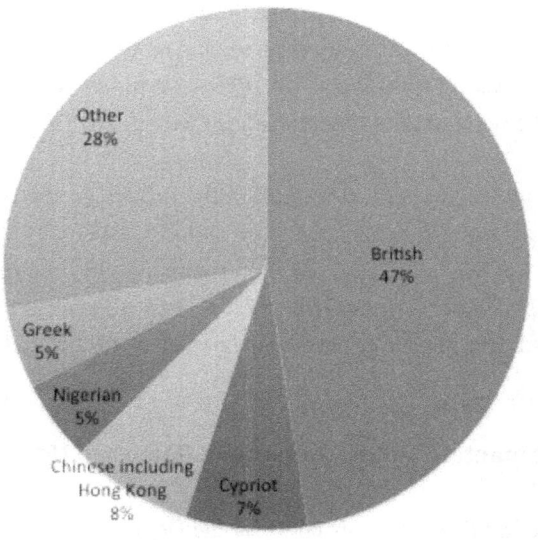

After the initial four contact hours, students do an in-class listening and speaking placement activity and either remain in F1 or move to F9. Both modules are taught together for all but five contact hours. We see from Figure 2 and Figure 3 that the placement of students resulted in most but not all UK and European students being placed in F1 and most but not all Chinese students being placed in F9.

Figure 3. IWLP F9, 2017-2018 (22 students)

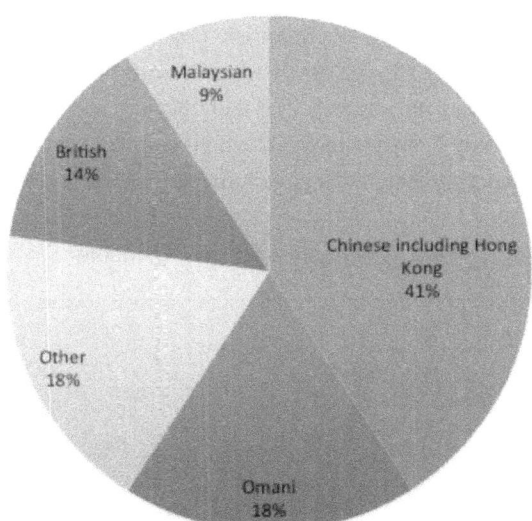

The contact hours for the F1 students were reduced to allow the F9 students to be taught on their own in small homogenous groups with focussed tutor support. During these workshop hours, the F9 students were able to practise and go back through set materials. Three of the five hours were timetabled early on in the course, Weeks 3, 4, and 8 of the autumn term. Knowing that extra support hours are available means tutors maintain the pace of the classes from the start.

The most innovative aspect of the F9 module is the new differentiated 'stepped' listening assessment. F9 students take two summative listening tests rather than just one. The final summative listening assessment is scaffolded for the F9 students (Figure 4).

IWLP learning outcomes are benchmarked against the CEFR but overlaid on these levels is the need to attribute a range of marks from distinction to fail. Students who reach the CEFR A1 may fail or achieve very low passes in listening because differentiating between the ranges of students means that the final listening has to include sections that exceed A1 level.

The students taking F1 sit only the final listening test worth 15% of the module mark. The learners taking F9 sit a first listening test in Week 4 of the spring term, worth 7.5%, which tests A1 material, and then they sit the final test with their F1 colleagues, worth only 7.5% for them. The final learning outcomes are achieved by both cohorts but the F9 students have more support along the way.

Figure 4. The scaffolded listening test for the F9 student

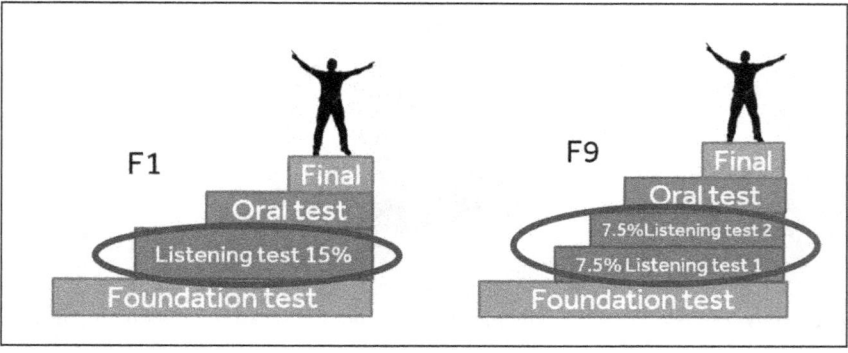

2.4. Phase 3 (January to April 2018)

Four students were funded to run a small project to collect student and tutor feedback on the new modules and to suggest further curriculum enhancement. They ran focus groups, analysed a questionnaire, and produced a written report on their findings. The outcomes are discussed below.

3. Outcomes and discussion

The feedback from the student mid- and end of module evaluations and focus groups shows that by offering the two new, co-taught modules, with targeted support, students were satisfied with the way we had addressed the issues of differentiation.

The support hours addressed the anxiety (Killick, 2017, p. 140) felt by the F9 students at the beginning of the course; a common comment from F9 students was that:

> "the smaller group lessons gave me a chance to practise and go over what I did not understand".

At the same time, we were successful in raising the pace of the lessons and ensuring an appropriate level of challenge and student engagement for the most able students. A typical learner's comment in the F1 end of module questionnaire was:

> "very engaging and interesting way of learning a language. Fast paced and effective".

Previously, there had always been a number of students who fed back that the pace was too slow. One tutor commented that it was actually easier to cover all the material with the whole cohort, despite the reduced hours, because of the supplementary F9 support teaching.

Overwhelmingly, students agreed that being taught together gives them a positive experience in the language class. Learners unanimously agreed that they should be taught together:

> "[k]eep the classes mixed as it is advantageous to both groups: a positive, interactive environment where students can help each other as well as develop themselves and [the mix] gives a culturally diverse class".

3.1. Feedback on assessment

We asked three questions:

- Did the extra support in listening skew the overall marks?
- Did the students feel that the differentiated assessment was unfair?
- How did the F9 students perceive the extra listening test?

The final listening test was the same for both cohorts, F1 and F9, so we were able to compare the marks. We made the final listening test more challenging, since for the F9 students it is now worth only 7.5% of their final mark. In the final listening test, the mean mark for the F1 students was 68% and for the F9 students it was 46%, a difference of more than 20% (Figure 5).

Figure 5. Comparison of F1 and F9 marks with only the final listening test

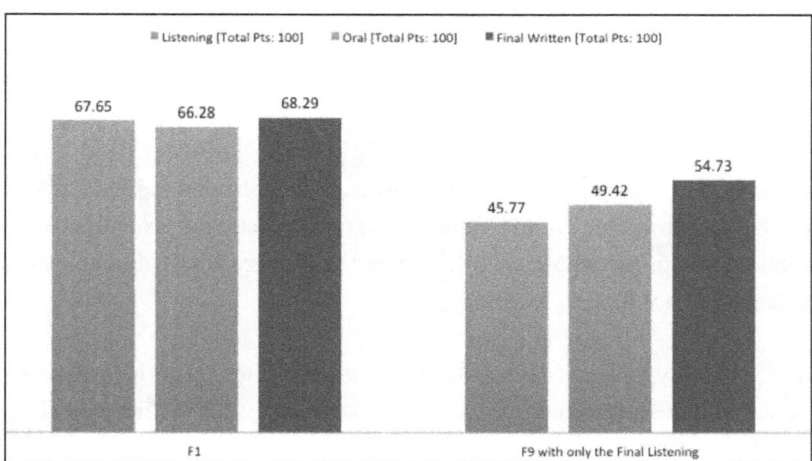

Combining the results of the two listening tests for F9 (each weighed as 7.5% of the module mark) raised the mean mark for the F9 students listening score to 57% (Figure 6).

The aim was to offer differentiated support to the two cohorts, but not to skew the overall results, and Figure 7 shows that the final mark distribution, for all skills, reflects the students' relative achievement on the course. This evidence satisfied staff that introducing the extra listening test and having different weightings for the final listening test still retained the students' ranking.

Figure 6.   The impact of two listening tests on the F9 overall marks

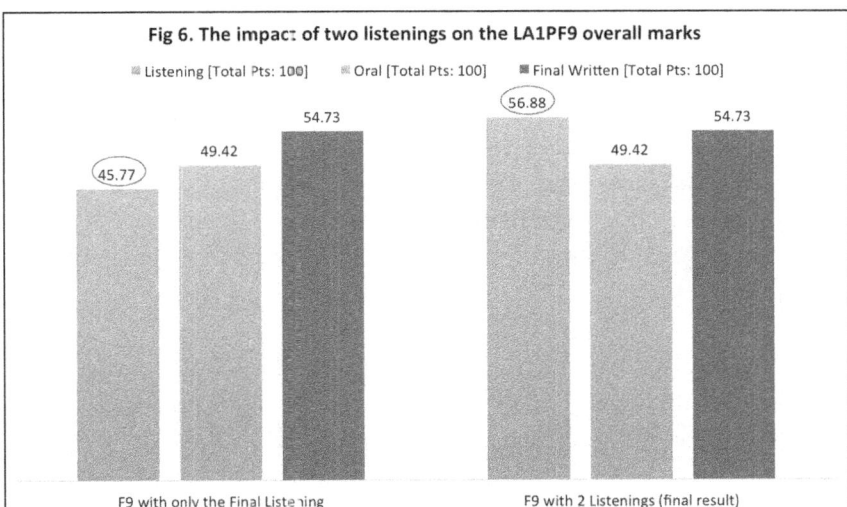

Figure 7.   Comparative overall mark distribution for the two modules

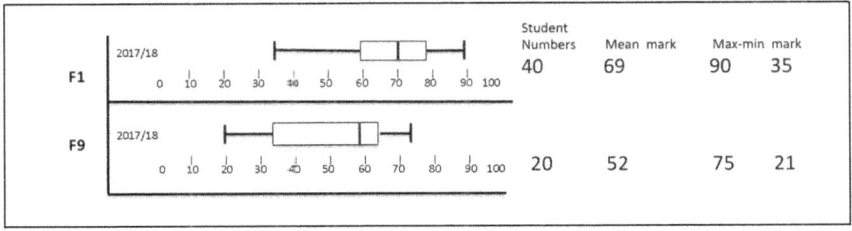

No student suggested that the listening weightings were unfair. In the group discussions, students recognised that, though they were all beginners, they were

in reality starting from very different points, given their cultural and linguistic diversity.

The F9 students might have felt that having two listening tests rather than one put them under extra pressure but apart from one, who felt it made no difference, this was not the case:

> "[b]ecause the modules are split into two and having another chance to experience the [listening] exam I felt less nervous about it".

3.2. What next?

In their report, students suggested further improvements. One was developing more listening practice materials on the virtual learning environment as part of the scheme of work for the F1 students in the hours that only F9 students come to the class.

The project evolved from focussing on speaking skills to giving more support for listening skills, both F1 and F9 students would still like more personalised tutor feedback on speaking as opposed to peer feedback.

4. Conclusion

Reducing student anxiety, recognising different starting points, and providing extra structured support has benefited both the weak and the strong students in the cohort. The former was anticipated and the latter less so. Undertaking this project, the teaching team has appreciated the value of working with students on course design and in future we will engage students at an earlier stage.

These A1 level language learners were very positive about the intercultural classrooms, even in a context where one group might perceive themselves at a disadvantage.

Mixed classes will always need careful management, but this intervention proved worthwhile for both students and lecturers.

Acknowledgements

Thanks to my IWLP French colleagues Alison Nicholson, Jenny Birk, and Sabine Martinez; the International Study and Language Institute and the PLaNT project funds, which both supported the project; and IWLP students Alex Lane, Maria Mitrou, Jiani Shen, and Ruiqi Wang.

References

Dlaska. A. (2013). The role of foreign language programmes in internationalising learning and teaching in higher education. *Teaching in Higher Education, 18*(3), 260-271. https://doi.org/10.1080/13562517.2012.696538

Gu, Q. (2010). Learning and growing in a 'foreign' context: intercultural experiences of international students. *Compare: A Journal of Comparative and International Education, 40*(1), 7-23. https://doi.org/10.1080/03057920903115983

Killick, D. (2017). *Internationalization and diversity in higher education. Implications for teaching, learning and assessment*. Palgrave.

UKCISA (2018). *International student statistics: UK higher education*. UK Council for International Student Affairs. https://www.ukcisa.org.uk/Research--Policy/Statistics/International-student-statistics-UK-higher-education

11. Improving feedback through computer-based language proficiency assessment

Tania Horák[1] and Elena Gandini[2]

Abstract

This paper reports on the proposed transfer of a paper-based English proficiency exam to an online platform. We discuss both the potential predetermined advantages, which were the impetus for the project, and also some emergent benefits, which prompted an in-depth analysis and reconceptualisation of the exam's role, which in turn we hope will promote positive washback as well as washforward. This change will be afforded through more granular feedback on student performance, which will be facilitated by the online platform.

Keywords: on-line testing, washback, washforward, English for academic purposes.

1. Introduction

The testing team at University of Central Lancashire (UCLan) produces a proficiency exam of English as a foreign language which is used in various situations, primarily to allow international students into programmes in their chosen discipline. It is known as the Test of English Language Level[3] (TELL) and

---

1. University of Central Lancashire, Preston, England; thorak@uclan.ac.uk; https://orcid.org/0000-0002-7461-8378

2. University of Central Lancashire, Preston, England; eamgandini@uclan.ac.uk; https://orcid.org/0000-0001-6341-4786

3. The UCLan-TELL is currently offered at level B1, B2, and C1 of the Common European Framework of Reference and it is a test of all four skills, each weighted equally.

How to cite this chapter: Horák, T., & Gandini, E. (2019). Improving feedback through computer-based language proficiency assessment. In N. Becerra, R. Biasini, H. Magedera-Hofhansl & A. Reimão (Eds), *Innovative language teaching and learning at university: a look at new trends* (pp. 95-103). Research-publishing.net. https://doi.org/10.14705/rpnet.2019.32.906

Chapter 11

is described as 'English for Academic Purposes (EAP)-light' in that it aims to cover the basic skill set students will draw on in their studies, albeit pitched at a relatively general level given that the exam can potentially be taken by a student of any discipline. Recently, a project was initiated to explore the viability of moving the exam to an online platform and we report on this in this article. This paper discusses the rationale for moving online and describes the test adaptation process and platform set up. We report here only on the receptive skills assessed on the UCLan-TELL, although the exam comprises all four skills. The piloting of the new computer-based exam is still ongoing and will be reported on at a later date.

2. Initial goals of moving online

There were a number of issues which acted as the impetus for investigating a new mode of delivery. The first was that, since the exam is used both in the UK and at partner institutions, reliability is compromised, somewhat inevitably, by a lack of parity of administration, which García Laborda (2007) suggests can be addressed through computerisation. It has long been acknowledged that there are various ways in which the consistency may be threatened (Lado, 1961), including variability in exam conditions (nature of invigilation, environmental factors, etc.). The UCLan-TELL is a relatively high-stakes exam in that it allows or denies access to further study, and thus as such, threats to reliability are not acceptable.

Another advantage of altering the mode of delivery was the possibility to improve security. There is always the possibility that exam integrity can be compromised, especially when operating at a distance from the UK campus, where it cannot be totally ensured who has access to the exam. As stated, the UCLan-TELL is a high-stakes exam for the candidates and consequently also for their tutors, as students' success tends to impact on them. Such tutors (and admin staff) are consequently in a difficult position due to the stakes involved. Anecdotally, we understand information has on occasion been passed on, even if with quite benign intentions, rather than constituting any nefarious activity.

This may even happen at a sub-conscious level, e.g. topics covered in revision lessons leading up to the exam. This compromises exam integrity and, thus, affects exam validity, and administration-related reliability. The online format avoids any possibility of prior access to test content and thus eliminates any possibility of passing on information about the papers.

A further driver to initiating this project was the future possibility, should the online version prove successful, of generating income by offering the exam to other institutions with similar needs, who may not have the resources to produce their own exam for the purpose of certifying international students' readiness for higher education. With this in mind, the salience of improvements in key areas such as reliability and a well-argued case for its validity would be paramount to make it an attractive product.

In addition, we envisage attractive features such as increased efficiency in scoring the objectively marked sections (reading and listening). On top of being inherently advantageous, this would reduce costs by obviating the need for human markers, or optical mark scanners and forms, as documented in the literature (see Chapelle & Voss, 2016). This might thus lead to a more marketable product, which would increase the chance of institutional project support.

3.   Further benefits

In the process of researching the platforms and in having to provide a sound rationale for what could potentially be a costly undertaking, further advantages came to light. The first of these was improved authenticity. While this is widely-interpreted, often in terms of "how well [the test] replicates real life in the tasks" (Fulcher, 2010, p. 98), we tried to address authenticity in relation to how far the means by which candidates accessed and produced text were in alignment with students' practice in general. The majority of students in higher education in the UK nowadays live their study lives mostly online (PWC, 2015); much, if not all, of their coursework is researched and submitted online, and the vast majority of their reading is online (Seyenney & Ross, 2008), as UCLan's Digital Shift project has widened the range and improved accessibility of the digital reading material. Therefore, bringing our English proficiency exam in line with this was felt to be a major advantage as it required students to read online and produce text online, given that this exam is most commonly used as "gatekeeping" (Davies et al., 1999, p. 66) for entry to higher education study in the UK.

Another emergent benefit, while not an immediate priority, was to better manage individual needs of students with certain specific learning difficulties. The inclusivity agenda, i.e. to maximise opportunity for all learners (NCEO, 2011), has for too long been left on a wish-list of future improvements regarding our exam, but being able to operationalise this effectively and reliably contributed to the list of positives for an online approach.

Above all, what became apparent through our investigation and development of ideas for adapting the exam and exploring possibilities in its new format was the potential to provide far better information to students on their performance. The online platform facilitates furnishing candidates with individualised information at a far more granular level than previously practically possible. Rather than an overall grade, or a grade per skill, the chosen online format allowed a breakdown of which sub-skills candidates demonstrated strengths or weaknesses in. For example, the feedback will highlight whether candidates demonstrated the ability to read for gist and detail, but not to infer meaning. Such information, combined with individualised prompts about how to improve in the weaker sub-skills, offers a formative element to what is usually perceived as summative assessment.

4. A paradigm shift?

In our experience, proficiency exams and other forms of summative assessment are viewed as an end point. They are frequently seen as an activity which needs to be pursued simply to allow entry to another phase of one's life (such as study, or a new job). They tend to foster a retrospective view of learning up to that point when the exam is taken. All in all, this approach can be summed up as being assessment *of* learning. In contrast, we felt the new candidate feedback format may allow a shift towards it simultaneously becoming assessment *for* learning (Gardner, 2012), seeing no good reason why the exam cannot straddle both functions.

Furnished with an individual personalised score profile and associated advice for how to improve areas of weakness, a candidate could utilise this to inform future language learning. The information supplied could help not only the candidate, but also any tutors who may be involved in their learning by taking on a diagnostic role to guide future study (Shohamy, 1992). On entering the higher education institution, international students will need to continue developing their language skills (Evans, Anderson, & Eggington, 2015) and a diagnosis of their needs should guide them in effectively selecting from the means of support available to them. Thus, the exam need not be only summative, but also formative and inform the next stage of further language development. In other words, the aim is for the promotion of this information to support positive washback, to influence study prior to the exam (Alderson & Wall, 1993), as well as addressing the exam's validity for its assigned purpose. Yet it also aims to enhance washforward (Andrews, Majer, Sargeant, & West, 2000), the effect of an exam on future learning. The format and content of high-stakes proficiency exams have been shown to influence aspects of the learning and teaching which takes place prior to that exam. Therefore, the feedback from performance on such exams can influence future learning and should be encouraged, e.g. addressing weaknesses identified by the exam outcomes.

5. How the individualised feedback is achieved

While the chosen platform allows for the generation of reports that give feedback to candidates, the default setup focusses on individual tasks. We felt that it would be more useful for candidates to receive feedback on their performance in the different skills and subskills coupled with suggestions on how to improve. For example, with regards to the receptive skills, this was achieved by tagging each item with a description (Figure 1) depicting the underlying sub-skills (Figure 2). The system analyses candidates' performances on all items that have the same tag and generates an automated email message detailing the scores achieved as well as explaining how improvements can be made on specific sub-skills and how this will reflect on academic language use.

Figure 1. Item tagging

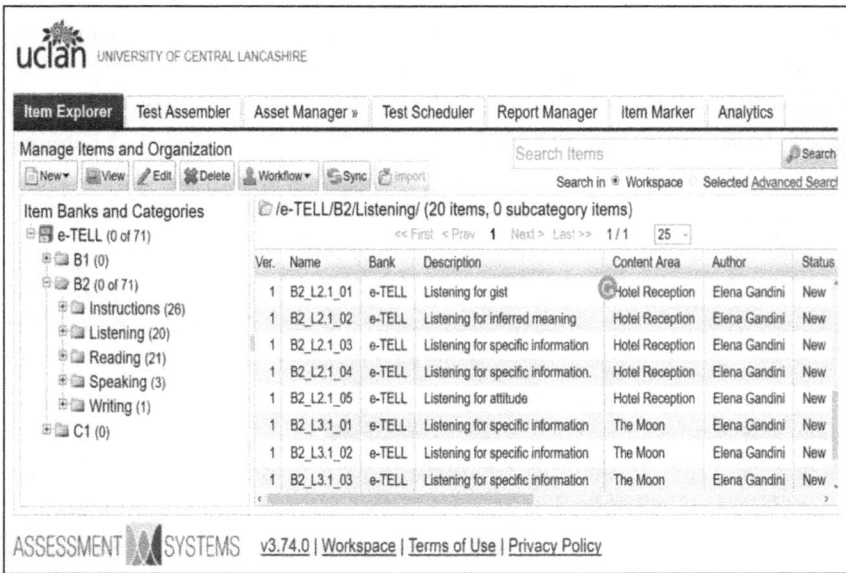

Our rationale for not using the default setup was that we wanted to help candidates think about their language ability in terms of specific skills and sub-skills, thus ultimately improving their understanding of what the exam is targeting and hence their assessment literacy. One way this could be improved would be to provide a visualisation of the candidate's individual profile, in the form of a chart depicting their performance in the specific subskills (Figure 3). This would enable candidates to better understand the areas that they need to focus on to improve their language ability.

Figure 2. Subskills tags

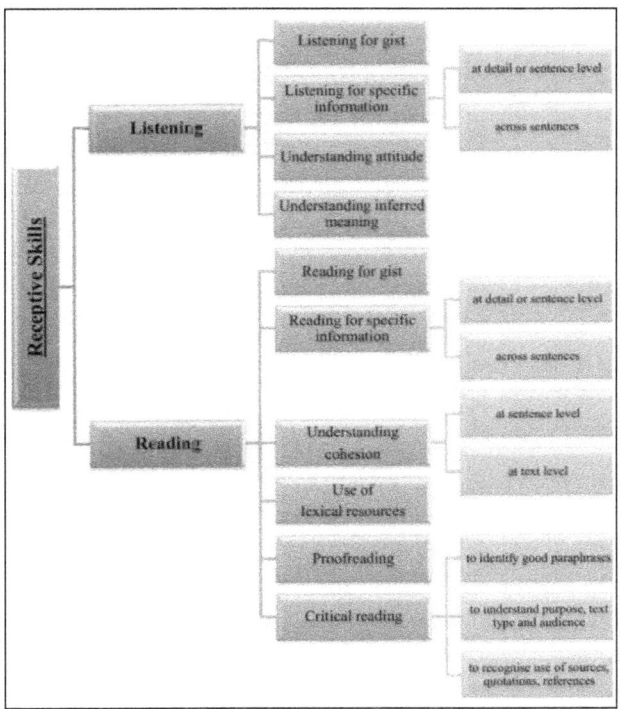

Figure 3. Example of candidate listening performance chart

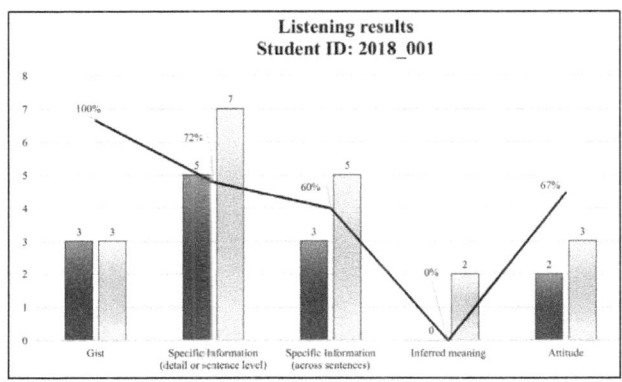

6. Conclusions

From an initial proposal to move our test to an online platform for administrative and business reasons arose a means to achieve potential pedagogically-focussed benefits. Although the project's future is not yet secured, meaning the exam may not move online, the process of investigation has been of great benefit, prompting us to instigate improvements in the current version.

References

Alderson, J. C., & Wall, D. (1993). Does washback exist? *Applied Linguistics, 14*(2), 115-129. https://doi.org/10.1093/applin/14.2.115

Andrews, J., Majer, J., Sargeant, D., & West, R. (2000). Reforming language examinations as classroom research: washback and washforward in a cluster of teacher training colleges in Poland. In M. Beaumont & T. O'Brien (Eds), *Collaborative research in second language education* (pp. 181-193). Trentham Books.

Chapelle, C. A., & Voss, E. (2016). 20 years of technology and language assessment in language learning & technology. *Language Learning & Technology, 20(2)*, 116-128.

Davies, A., Brown, A., Elder, C., Hill, K., Lumley, T., & McNamara, T. (1999). *Dictionary of language testing. Studies in Language Testing 7*. Cambridge University Press.

Evans, N. W., Anderson, N. J., & Eggington, W. G. (2015). *ESL readers and writers in higher education. understanding challenges, providing support*. Routledge. https://doi.org/10.4324/9781315762654

Fulcher, G. (2010). *Practical language testing*. Hodder Education

García Laborda, J. (2007). On the net: introducing standardized EFL/ESL exams. *Language Learning & Technology, 11(2)*, 3-9.

Gardner, J. (2012). *Assessment and learning* (2nd ed.). SAGE Publications Ltd.

Lado, R. (1961). *Language testing*. Longman.

NCEO. (2011). Don't forget accommodations! Five questions to ask when moving to technology-based assessments. *NCEO Brief April 2011(1)*, University of Minnesota, National Venter on Educational Outcomes.

PWC. (2015). *The 2018 digital university. Staying relevant in the digital age*. https://www.pwc.co.uk/assets/pdf/the-2018-digital-university-staying-relevant-in-the-digital-age.pdf

Seyenney, P., & Ross, L., (2008). The library is dead, long live the library! The practice of academic librarianship and the digital revolution. *The Journal of Academic Librarianship, 34*(2), 145-152. https://doi.org/10.1016/j.acalib.2007.12.006

Shohamy, E. (1992). Beyond proficiency testing: a diagnostic feedback testing model for assessing foreign language learning. *The Modern Language Journal, 76*(4), 513-521. https://doi.org/10.1111/j.1540-4781.1992.tb05402.x

12. Student-led grammar revision: empowering first year Spanish beginner students to facilitate their own learning

Nadezhda Bonelli[1] and Anna Nibbs[2]

Abstract

This paper presents an innovative project-based learning activity meant to support language beginner students to develop, via their core curriculum, five enterprise capabilities (*authentic problem-solving; innovation and creativity; risk-taking; taking action;* and *true collaboration*), formulated at the University of Sheffield after Quality Assurance Agency (QAA) guidance and based on best UK government policy and sector practice. Within the written language component of a first year Spanish language beginners' course in Hispanic studies, students undertake an optional formative exercise towards their examination preparation: preparing and delivering presentations on key aspects of the Spanish language to be employed firstly with classmates and subsequently with Year 9 to Year 12 (Y9-Y12) students in local schools, responding to requirements developed collaboratively by school teachers and the language tutor.

Keywords: empowering students, learning capabilities.

---

1. University of Sheffield, Sheffield, Eng and; n.bonelli@sheffield.ac.uk

2. University of Sheffield, Sheffield, Eng and; a.nibbs@sheffield.ac.uk

How to cite this chapter: Bonelli, N., & Nibbs, A. (2019). Student-led grammar revision: empowering first year Spanish beginner students to facilitate their own learning. In N. Becerra, R. Biasini, H. Magedera-Hofhansl & A. Reimão (Eds), *Innovative language teaching and learning at university: a look at new trends* (pp. 105-114). Research-publishing.net. https://doi.org/10.14705/rpnet.2019.32.907

Chapter 12

1. Introduction

This paper presents an innovative approach to tackling Spanish grammar concepts which are traditionally problematic for English native speakers. It was developed in response to the remarkable commitment and dedication of first-year Spanish beginner students (approx. 25-30 annually) on an undergraduate Hispanic studies degree at the University of Sheffield who wished to apply their Spanish language knowledge beyond the classroom environment.

The first-year (Framework for Higher Education Qualification Level 4; 'Level 1' within the institution) beginners' course is conceived for students with no prior experience of Spanish. Students are expected to reach a Common European Framework of Reference for languages (CEFR) A2+/B1 level in Spanish via a programme of intensive language modules focussed on grammar and written language, designed to substantially narrow the gap between beginners and post-A Level peers by the end of their second year. As in many UK institutions, the final year of study (fourth year, post-year abroad) makes no distinction between former beginner ('Level 1B') and post-A Level ('Level 1A') students.

The project addresses the needs of Level 1B students, supporting them not only to achieve course objectives and to prepare for credit-bearing assessed presentations during their second and fourth years of study, but also to experience and to develop capabilities that potentially enhance subject learning, academic skills development, and employability.

2. Context

The project was underpinned by a number of pedagogical theories and approaches, namely *Enterprise Education, Project-Based Learning*, and *Service Learning*, as detailed below.

The University of Sheffield defines curricular enterprise education as the opportunity for students to develop five key enterprise capabilities: *authentic problem-solving; innovation and creativity; risk-taking; taking action*; and *true collaboration*[3] (Riley, 2017). These emerged from research conducted among teaching colleagues (e.g. Riley, 2017) and an extensive history of embedding enterprise into subject disciplines, building on best sector practice (EEUK, 2018), government policy (Wilson, 2012; Witty, 2013; Young, 2014), and QAA (2012, 2018) guidance on enterprise and entrepreneurship education, which recommends that enterprise education responsibilities extend beyond business schools and careers services, and that enterprise skills are relevant to *all* subject disciplines.

Finally, enterprise education often incorporates project-based learning and service learning, as demonstrated by Rodriguez-Falcon and Yoxall (2010) and Sheffield Hallam University's Venture Matrix scheme (EEUK, 2015).

The present project, being formative, lacks some accepted service learning features (Bringle & Hatcher, 1996; Harkavy & Hartley, 2010), but is informed by such approaches. Its originality lies in the level of study at which such an activity occurs. Successful collaborative projects involving language beginners include activities such as writing wikis (Castañeda & Cho, 2013) or language dictionaries (Lopez, 2016), but unlike this project, these have not directly involved external partners.

Activities involving schools or community partners (Barreneche & Ramos-Flores, 2013; Pellettieri, 2011; Tocaimaza-Hatch, 2018; University of Leeds, n.d.) often occur post-first year. Language students in most UK institutions undertake a year abroad after their second year of study – another 'embedded enterprise' languages initiative at the same institution (University of Sheffield, 2018) occurs after this point.

In these examples, students are expected to have achieved considerably greater levels of target language competency before embarking on external engagement activity than was expected of students on the project in question.

---

3. See supplementary material, appendix 1; https://research-publishing.box.com/s/6w2bh2y07r9v37nhx4rw8pdq17n24132

3. The student-led grammar revision project

The project involves a mid-semester revision activity (one of three formative assessments completed during the second semester) involving interaction with students and teachers from a local school and a staged series of scaffolded project activities, undertaken as preparation for an end-of-semester formal written language assessment. Students receive indicative marks, which do not contribute to the final course mark, and formative feedback to support their subsequent learning and development, as well as informal feedback at various points throughout the project.

In pairs or threes, students have three weeks to prepare and deliver a 30- to 35-minute presentation on a specific Spanish grammatical structure, as shown in Figure 1.

Figure 1. Elements of the student presentation

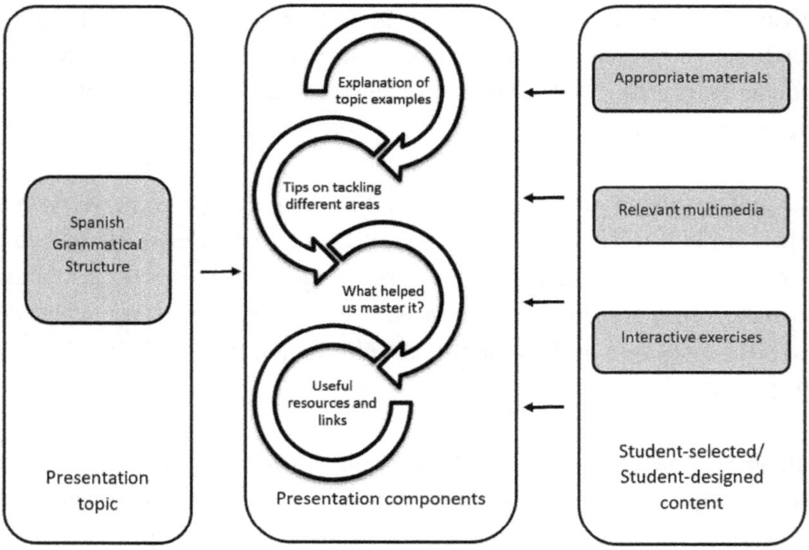

Students are enabled to develop enterprise capabilities as follows:

Authentic problem solving

- Consolidating, building upon, and applying language understanding to address, within constraints, Y9-Y12 students' specific learning needs.
- Exploring techniques and strategies.
- Continually reflecting upon their own learning approach.

Innovation and creativity

- Freedom to design presentations using educational tools of their choosing.
- Identifying and implementing effective, engaging ways of tackling the topic, using approaches appealing to young audiences.

Risk-taking

- Many students' first experience of presenting to an external audience.
- Exceeding comfort zone at a relatively early stage of study.
- Uncertainties over audience reactions and responses.

Taking action

- Self-directed, student-led design, development and delivery.
- Pro-actively addressing intended audience needs within time constraints.

True collaboration

- Adjusting presentation designs in response to class peer feedback.
- Engaging dynamically with, and creating value for, a community.
- Presentation materials provided to schools for further use in revising specific areas of the language, examination preparation and facilitating understanding.

Students are closely supported by their tutor throughout each of the project stages, as illustrated in Figure 2.

Chapter 12

Figure 2. Project stages and input/support

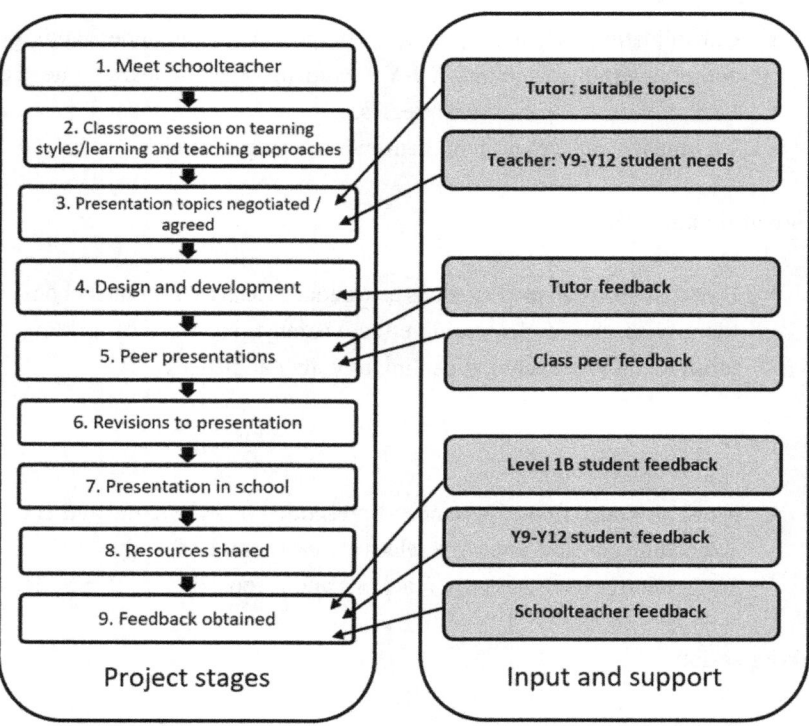

In three years of running the project with annual cohorts of 25-30, only two participating students did not fully complete it, undertaking the necessary design and preparation work in their groups and presenting in class to peers, but for personal reasons opting out of presenting in schools. In both cases, their fellow group members managed this aspect.

4. Outcomes

Project feedback was obtained through three separate questionnaires completed by Level 1B students, school students, and teachers following the presentations in schools[4]. Thereafter, Level 1B students and the tutor discussed their responses and the project as a whole, whilst the tutor had further discussions with participating schoolteachers.

Teachers found presentations stimulating, encouraging, and beneficial for their students, as grammar is explained from the perspective of native English speakers close to their students' own educational experience. Y9-Y12 students and their teachers have access to presentation materials as an ongoing resource.

The project has become an attractive proposition to prospective students and families at open days, inspiring local school outreach activities within the same department. It is also an excellent experience for students considering teaching assistantships as part of their year abroad. Such benefits reprise those of earlier 'embedded enterprise' developments at the institution, including the All About Linguistics project for first-year English Language and Linguistics students (Wood, 2014a, 2014b).

5. Discussion

A number of findings from the aforementioned student questionnaires, and from the tutor's observations, are worthy of further consideration. For instance, the approach presented is relatively uncharted territory for university-level beginner language teaching, but builds upon work undertaken elsewhere within the same institution, demonstrating transferability, across disciplines, of approaches already proven successful. Furthermore, in being conducted as a formative exercise, it demonstrates how a small-scale initiative can have considerable impact without overhaul of existing assessment methods, wholesale module re-design, or the resourcing demands such processes would entail.

Some of the challenges had to do with the less confident students as well as with the tutor's increased workload, and they were successfully overcome by

---
4. See supplementary material, appendices 2 to 5; https://research-publishing.box.com/s/6w2bh2y07r9v37nhx4rw8pdq17n24132

Chapter 12

encouraging, supporting, and closely working with less confident students, and finally by allocating additional hours within the Level 1B Spanish Beginners course into the tutor's teaching timetable.

Minimal negative feedback (two responses) concerned preparation putting additional pressure on an already full timetable, and teammates' lack of participation. As student feedback was anonymous, the course tutor addressed negative feelings in class, exploring with the students how best to avoid these.

Students agreed that for future group work they would try to keep within time limits, distribute work evenly, and take better responsibility for allocated roles. Managing group dynamics and dealing with difficult teamwork experiences are challenges frequently experienced in employment; thus, the practice of addressing such challenges through an authentic learning experience has potential employability benefits.

One limitation is the extent to which project outcomes are transferable beyond the cohorts discussed. It would be valuable to compare it to similar initiatives (as they emerge), and explore longer-term impacts on student progression and skills development.

6. Conclusions

Beyond simple language revision, this project brings a stimulating, authentic element (Riley, 2017) to the beginners' course through meaningful community connections, and students have the opportunity to create and innovate, developing skills applicable throughout their studies. In our experience, students deeply value what is often their first experience of applying subject knowledge outside the classroom.

The tutor has a key role in liaising with schools and supporting students throughout the project. Likewise, the continuous support, motivation, and encouragement provided to less confident students is of paramount importance.

Here, *all* students are empowered and trusted as teachers. It is gratifying to see them embrace the project and succeed in its execution. The tutor plans to continue the project at Level 1B Spanish Beginners and to investigate the possibility of taking the idea to other language courses within the University.

We conclude that this exercise enhances students' engagement with their course, university, and community, and leads to a more rewarding, enjoyable teaching experience, concurring, as Reinders (2010) suggests, that it is important, as teachers, to set activities to encourage students to find ways to move beyond the classroom and incorporate new knowledge into their lives.

Acknowledgements

The project was first realised thanks to an Enterprise Curriculum Development Grant awarded by the University of Sheffield Enterprise Academy in 2015.

References

Barreneche, G., & Ramos-Flores, H. (2013). Integrated or isolated experiences? Considering the role of service-learning in the Spanish language curriculum. *Hispania, 96*(2), 215-228. https://doi.org/10.1353/hpn.2013.0063

Bringle, R. G., & Hatcher, J. A. (1996). Implementing service learning in higher education. *Journal of Higher Education, 67*(2), 221-239. https://doi.org/10.2307/2943981

Castañeda, D. A., & Cho, M. H. (2013). The role of wiki writing in learning Spanish grammar. *Computer Assisted Language Learning, 26*(4), 334-349.

EEUK. (2015). *Venture matrix. Enhancing the curriculum (ETC) toolkit.* Enterprise Educators UK. https://www.etctoolkit.org.uk/enterprise-case-studies-library/venture-matrix-qaa-1-2-3-4-5-6-7/

EEUK. (2018). *Advice and resources.* Enterprise Educators UK. https://www.enterprise.ac.uk/share/#advice

Harkavy, I., & Hartley, D. (2010). Pursuing Franklin's dream: philosophical and historical roots of service-learning. *American Journal of Community Psychology, 46*(3-4), 418-427.

Lopez, N. (2016). A case study: writing a Spanish dictionary as a collaborative task among beginner students. *The Language Learning Journal, 44*(1), 52-73. https://doi.org/10.1080/09571736.2012.731699

Pellettieri, J. (2011). Measuring language-related outcomes of community-based learning in intermediate Spanish courses. *Hispania, 94*(2), 285-302.

QAA. (2012). *Enterprise and entrepreneurship education: guidance for UK higher education providers, September 2012*. Quality Assurance Agency for Higher Education.

QAA. (2018). *Enterprise and entrepreneurship education: guidance for UK higher education providers, January 2018*. Quality Assurance Agency for Higher Education.

Reinders, H. (2010). Towards a classroom pedagogy for learner autonomy: a framework of independent language skills. *Australian Journal of Teacher Education, 35*(5), 40-55. https://doi.org/10.14221/ajte.2010v35n5.4

Riley, A. (2017). Training the trainers for embedding enterprise in diverse curricula. *Paper presented at the Institute for Small Business and Entrepreneurship (ISBE) Conference, Belfast, UK, 8-9 November 2017*.

Rodriguez-Falcon, E., & Yoxall, A. (2010). Service learning experiences: a way forward in teaching engineering students? *Engineering Education, 5*(2), 59-68.

Tocaimaza-Hatch, C. C. (2018). Speaking is doing and doing is learning: vocabulary learning in service-learning. *Journal of Spanish Language Teaching, 5*(1), 66-80.

University of Leeds (n.d.). *Students into schools*. https://www.leeds.ac.uk/info/128010/teachers_and_advisors/61/students_into_schools

University of Sheffield (2018). *German for enterprise*. https://www.sheffield.ac.uk/german/undergraduates/enterprise/about

Wilson, T. (2012). *A review of business–university collaboration*. BIS. https://assets.publishing.service.gov.uk/government/uploads/system/uploads/attachment_data/file/32383/12-610-wilson-review-business-university-collaboration.pdf

Witty, A. (2013). *Encouraging a British invention revolution: Sir Andrew Witty's review of universities and growth*. BIS.

Wood, G. C. (2014a). Towards an A-to-Z of enterprise in the curriculum: a case study all about linguistics. *Paper presented at EEUK Best Practice Event, Cardiff, 26 March 2014*.

Wood, G. C. (2014b). Real enrichment, real engagement, real projects: Google Apps to enhance the student learning experience. *Paper presented at Google Apps in Learning and Teaching Workshop, Sheffield Hallam University, 7 March 2014*.

Young, L. (2014). *Enterprise for all: the relevance of enterprise in education*. BIS.

13. Awareness poster campaign for the development of presentation skills in Spanish

Elia Lorena López[1]

Abstract

This paper describes a project-based oral activity trialled with Year 1 and Year 2 students of the Spanish Degree Programme at the University of York. The objective of the activity aimed to develop students' speaking confidence through the completion of an authentic task based on the concept of authentic assessment. This task was implemented during the academic year 2017-18 and consisted of students developing poster campaigns with a slogan and hashtag that they would subsequently justify during their presentation. The task had outstanding results as students benefited from practising a range of practical skills and reported it to be a very rewarding experience. As a result, it is intended that this activity will now be integrated in oral summative assessments for the modules in which this task was trialled.

Keywords: oral presentations, authentic assessment, professional skills, group assessment.

1. Introduction

The objective of the formative oral-based activity described in this paper was to encourage students to develop the precise, organised, and effective oral skills

---

1. University of York, York, England; lorena.lopez@york.ac.uk

How to cite this chapter: López, E. L. (2019). Awareness poster campaign for the development of presentation skills in Spanish. In N. Becerra, R. Biasini, H. Magedera-Hofhansl & A. Reimão (Eds), *Innovative language teaching and learning at university: a look at new trends* (pp. 115-122). Research-publishing.net. https://doi.org/10.14705/rpnet.2019.32.908

much valued in the current labour market. The task, set out for the core Spanish language modules in Years 1 and 2 of the Spanish Degree Programme at the University of York, involved the design of a fictitious advertising campaign by designing a poster accompanied by a slogan and a hashtag. Students not only planned and designed a poster campaign, but they also presented the rationale behind their project to the class audience. This second part requires the use of business pitch skills with a focus on persuasive language. Students were given flexibility to make use of a wide range of technological and social media tools, hence allowing them a wide range of creativity and individual skills.

By using a communicative language teaching approach, University of York tutors model the production of meaningful verbal communication. Students who attend Spanish language modules are fully immersed in the target language during contact times. This approach is also extended to other core modules of the Spanish degree programmes such as the Spanish Language and Society I and II modules. In this module, students are introduced to "a variety of written and aural materials"[2] to reinforce the development of linguistic competencies in order to achieve a high level of fluency and accuracy in the production of written and spoken Spanish.

Furthermore, students' oral production in seminars is supported by continuous interaction between the tutor and students' peers, who prompt them to use relevant discursive markers, debating phrases and conversational connectors, to name but a few linguistic characteristics. The existing literature has highlighted the positive effect of repetition on fluency and language acquisition. This leads to an increased rate of speaking, a greater level of vocabulary retention, and on building confidence (Brooks & Wilson, 2014). Also, Prichard and Ferreira (2014), by citing Baddeley (1990) and Logan (1988), highlight that repetition of a task allows for skills to move from controlled to automatic processing and that this has been proven to be the case for language learning in relation to accuracy and fluency.

---

2. https://www.york.ac.uk/language/current/undergraduates/modules/2011-12/s12i/

Another reason for starting this project was the increasingly fierce competition in the labour market requiring highly articulate graduates; nowadays numerous reports (The Economist Intelligence Unit, 2015; World Bank, 2018; World Economic Forum, 2016) suggest that an effective use of the language has proven to be a powerful tool that makes individuals stand out. For example, in a US study, Sims Peterson (1997) found evidence that effective communication skills have significantly influenced employers' hiring decisions, especially in the last 30 years, and are therefore considered essential for success.

Finally, and central to this proposed project, is the concept of authentic assessment which entails the replication of tasks, challenges, and standards of execution carried out by real-life professionals (Wiggins, 1989). These "forms of assessment in which students are asked to perform 'real-world' tasks that demonstrate meaningful application of essential knowledge and skills" (Mueller, 2016 in Thurab-Nkhosi, Williams, & Mason-Roberts, 2018, p. 652) support student confidence and course engagement. Furthermore, students are more able to use different types of skills and therefore improve their quality of learning and competencies (Newman, Secada, & Wehlage, 1995 in Thurab-Nkhosi et al., 2018; Wiggins, 1990) and on top of this, their chances of becoming more employable (Villarroel et al., 2017).

2. Method

2.1. Task instruction

During one teaching week, 47 students were put in teams of three. They were instructed to design an awareness campaign on a social issue. Students could then embark on the task of designing a poster, a slogan, and a hashtag for the campaign on a social issue from a list of topics to choose from that were part of the modules' syllabi, for example, endangered languages, catcalling, and discrimination in Latin America. These topics were then presented in class. Subsequently, they pitched their poster in approximately five minutes with one student explaining the rationale for the whole campaign, another justifying the poster design, and the third mostly being responsible for answering questions from the audience.

It is worth clarifying three aspects related to the task; firstly, no specific grammatical target structures were required but emphasis was put on the need for the campaign to send an impactful message; secondly, choice of software for designing the poster was left at students' discretion. Finally, the fact that the roles assigned to the three members of the team were different meant that each student was going to invest more time and effort on a specific aspect of the project, therefore, they each developed specific skills. This, however, was not perceived as a problem given that students had to consider that in every day work, and that teamwork requires that people draw on diverse skills (The Higher Education Academy, 2014). Furthermore, the object of the evaluation (formatively at this trial stage) by means of the usual speaking skills criteria plus added criteria for poster design, was the outcome itself. This was a way to guarantee the reliability of individual contributions. Twenty percent of the total module mark was assessed through peer assessment.

2.2. Preliminary work

Students received theoretical and practical preparation on the key skills for the development of this task prior to the release of the final task instruction. Information was presented to them and examples of advertising campaigns and awareness posters were then discussed in class. Some of the other knowledge and abilities required for the task had already been covered as part of the course syllabus, for example, presentation structure, the use of body language in presentations, etc. In particular, the students were prepared with the following skills in preparation for the task:

- objective of advertising campaigns,

- poster design,

- characteristics of effective posters (clear and easy to read, prioritising information, sending a clear message, not needing verbal explanation, correct grammar and spelling, inviting to viewer),

- visual presentation of argument,

- producing focussed, purposeful, meaningful, and structured business-like pitches and viewpoints, typically following the Point + Evidence + Explanation method, an essay-writing technique widely used in UK GSCE and A Level education (both in writing and orally),

- effective pitching skills by considering audience, location, duration, structure, message, body language, etc., and

- use of persuasive language.

3. Results and discussion

After the presentations had been assessed, students were surveyed for feedback on their perceptions of this authentic task and out of 47 students, 26 responded. In terms of the usefulness of the task, the general perception of students was that they found the task useful and enjoyable. The evaluation showed that 60% agreed that the exercise helped them gain specific knowledge on a wide range of language and employability skills; 35% 'more or less' agreed to this, and 5% reported not finding it particularly useful.

When asked to provide details as to the type of knowledge and skills they believed to have gained, it was clear that skills gain was predominant in comparison with the actual knowledge gained. The key skills that they mentioned were in order of recurrence: (1) team skills by doing group work, i.e. dividing up tasks, organisational skills; (2) presentation skills, i.e. summarising information, speaking in public; (3) designing posters, i.e. using eye-catching, effective, and emotive images; (4) conveying impactful messages; and (5) learning thematic-specific vocabulary in Spanish. In terms of knowledge, the great majority found in-depth research on specific themes to be useful.

A powerful message was that 85% of students responding reported that they had enjoyed working on this assignment. This shows that engaging with realistic tasks and letting learners showcase their varied skills contributes to student engagement, especially if they value these activities as similar to the ones they have to complete in their future jobs (Villarroel et al., 2017). Furthermore, 35% found this undertaking challenging, 40% found it dynamic, and 10% perceived it as exhausting. What students mostly enjoyed included (in terms of recurrence): (1) designing the poster, (2) designing the slogan, (3) reading about the topic, and (4) presenting the poster. Having the presentation part not at the top preferred activity does not come as a surprise given the high levels of anxiety that language oral tests provoke in students, according to the literature (Philips, 1992; see also Aleksandrzak, 2011; Scott, 1986; Von Worde, 2003). Interestingly, what they enjoyed the least included: (1) working in groups as students found it difficult to find enough time outside class or due to individual workload, (2) trying to fit all relevant information into a poster format, and (3) the presentation itself, which confirms the literature on second language test anxiety.

Other findings include that in the open comments section of the feedback, students have felt empowered after carrying out this task as they were able to showcase their creativity and unique skills. For instance, many had the opportunity to use their skills with digital tools, as the majority of groups used Publisher for the poster design while the rest used Microsoft Word and PowerPoint. Derived from that, students also reported to have achieved greater class cohesion and increased peer interaction, not only with their group members but also with the rest of the class as they were all in the same challenging situation.

4. Conclusion

The idea of introducing a project-based learning activity for students originated from the need of tasks based on real-life professional practice. Many graduates go on to find employment in the advertising or marketing sector where pitching skills are essential, and as most employers value communication skills and team work, the design of an awareness poster and articulating the rationale behind it seemed ideal.

The survey at the end of the task showed that it allowed them to gain both knowledge and skills and that they find it highly enjoyable as an assessment. While many found group work a useful skill to develop, they also found the experience challenging due to having to negotiate not only skills but also schedules with their peers. All in all, various skills in the target language were gained such as summarising, organising, and delivering clear and meaningful information within a specific amount of time.

Also, students reported that they enjoyed planning and executing the task because they felt that they gained new knowledge and professional skills. More importantly, the great majority reported feeling empowered as they were able to showcase individual skills and strengths to their peers. For these reasons, this task will be embedded into the summative oral exams of the modules described of the Spanish core modules in Year 1 and Year 2, and as the assessment has been welcomed widely, other language modules in the Department of Language and Linguistics will replicate this exercise in the short term.

References

Aleksandrzak, M. (2011). Problems and challenges in teaching and learning speaking at advanced learning. *Glottodidactica, 37*, 37-48.

Baddeley, A. (1990). *Human memory*. Lawrence Erlbaum Associates.

Brooks, G., & Wilson, J. (2014). Using oral presentations to improve students' English language skills. *Kwansei Gakuin University Humanities Review, 19*(1), 199-212.

Logan, G. D. (1988). Toward an instance theory of automatization. *Psychological Review, 95*(4), 492–527. https://doi.org/10.1037/0033-295X.95.4.492

Mueller, J. (2016). *Authentic assessment toolbox*. http://jfmueller.faculty.noctrl.edu/toolbox/whatisit.htm

Newmann, F., Secada, W., & Wehlage, G. (1995). A guide to authentic instruction and assessment: vision, standards and scoring. ASCD.

Peterson, M. S. (1997). Personnel interviewers' perceptions of the importance and adequacy of applicants' communication skills. *Communication Education, 46*(4), 287-291. https://doi.org/10.1080/03634529709379102

Phillips, E. M. (1992). The effects of language anxiety on students' oral test performance and attitudes. *Modern Language Journal, 76*, 14-2.

Prichard, C., & Ferreira, D. (2014). The effects of poster presentations and class presentations on low-proficiency learners. *TESOL Journal, 5*(1), 172-185. https://doi.org/10.1002/tesj.131

Scott, M. L. (1986). Student affective reactions to oral language tests. *Language Testing, 3*(1), 99-118.

The Economist Intelligence Unit. (2015). *Driving the skills agenda: preparing students for the future.* https://static.googleusercontent.com/media/edu.google.com/pt-BR//pdfs/skills-of-the-future-report.pdf

The Higher Education Academy. (2014). *Group Work.* https://www.heacademy.ac.uk/system/files/group_work.pdf

Thurab-Nkhosi, D., Williams, G., & Mason-Roberts, M. (2018). Achieving confidence in competencies through authentic assessment. *Journal of Management Development, 37*(8), 652-662. https://doi.org/10.1108/JMD-12-2017-0413

Villarroel, V., Bloxham, S., Bruna, D., Bruna, C., & Herrera-Seda, C. (2017). Authentic assessment: creating a blueprint for course design. *Assessment and Evaluation in Higher Education, 43*(5), 840-854.

Von Worde, R. (2003). *Students' perspectives on foreign language anxiety. Inquiry, 8*(1), 36-49.

Wiggins, G. (1989). A true test: toward more authentic and equitable assessment. *Phi Delta Kappan, 70*(9), 703-713.

Wiggins, G. (1990). The case for authenticassessment. *Practical Assessment, Research &Evaluation, 2*(2), 1-3. http://PAREonline.net/getvn.asp?v=2&n=2

World Bank. (2018). Measuring skills demanded by employers: skills toward employment and productivity (STEP) (English). *Jobs Notes, 5.* http://documents.worldbank.org/curated/en/210071526072991842/Measuring-skills-demanded-by-employers-skills-toward-employment-and-productivity-STEP

World Economic Forum. (2016, January). *The future of jobs: employment, skills and workforce strategy for the fourth industrial revolution.* http://www3.weforum.org/docs/WEF_Future_of_Jobs.pdf

Author index

B
Becerra, Nelson v, 1
Biasini, Rosalba v, 1
Bohm, Anke xi, 3, 53
Bonelli, Nadezhda xi, 4, 105

D
Di Maio, Fabrizio xi, 3, 45

F
Federici, Theresa xii, 3, 37

G
Gallagher-Brett, Angela xii, 3, 29
Gandini, Elena xii, 4, 95

H
Herrero, Carmen xii, 2, 19
Horák, Tania xiii, 4, 95

K
Koeper-Saul, Veronika xiii, 3, 53
Kurose, Mikiko xiii, 3, 63

L
Li, Miao xiii, 4, 73
López, Elia Lorena xiii, 4, 115

M
Magedera-Hofhansl, Hanna v, 1
Masuhara, Hitomi xiv, 2, 9
Mossmann, Christian xiv, 3, 53

N
Nader, Alison xiv, 4, 83
Nibbs, Anna xiv, 4, 105

R
Reimão, Ana v, 1

www.ingramcontent.com/pod-product-compliance
Lightning Source LLC
Chambersburg PA
CBHW031633160426
43196CB00006B/398